THE SOVIET DESTRUCTION OF ARMY GROUP SOUTH

CASEMATE | ILLUSTRATED

C CASEMATE | ILLUSTRATED

THE SOVIET DESTRUCTION OF ARMY GROUP SOUTH

UKRAINE AND SOUTHERN POLAND, 1943–45

IAN BAXTER

![CASEMATE | ILLUSTRATED]

CIS0029

Print Edition: ISBN 978-1-63624-262-0
Digital Edition: ISBN 978-1-63624-263-7

Design by Battlefield Design
Printed and bound by Megaprint, Turkey

CASEMATE PUBLISHERS (US)
Telephone (610) 853-9131
Fax (610) 853-9146
Email: casemate@casematepublishers.com
www.casematepublishers.com

CASEMATE PUBLISHERS (UK)
Telephone (0)1226 734350
Email: casemate-uk@casematepublishers.co.uk
www.casematepublishers.co.uk

All photos contained in this book are derived from archival sources, including the US National Archives and Records Administration, Library of Congress, Bundesarchiv, and the US Military History Institute, unless otherwise noted.

Author's note: Geographic names are given as they were during World War II and do not reflect current usage.

Title page image: A knocked-out T-34-76 M1943 blocks the path of a Marder, Ukraine, summer 1944.
Contents page map: Soviet operations, July 17–December 1, 1943. (U.S. Army)
Contents page image: A Soviet 120mm mortar crew in action.

Acknowledgements: I wish to thank my artist Johnny Shumate for some of the illustrations in this book. I also want to thank my armored artist Oliver Missing for his time and expertise in producing some fine and well-detailed German and Soviet tanks, and including producing the maps. Please find Oliver's vast selection of illustrations at his "Engines of WW2" site www.o5m6.de.

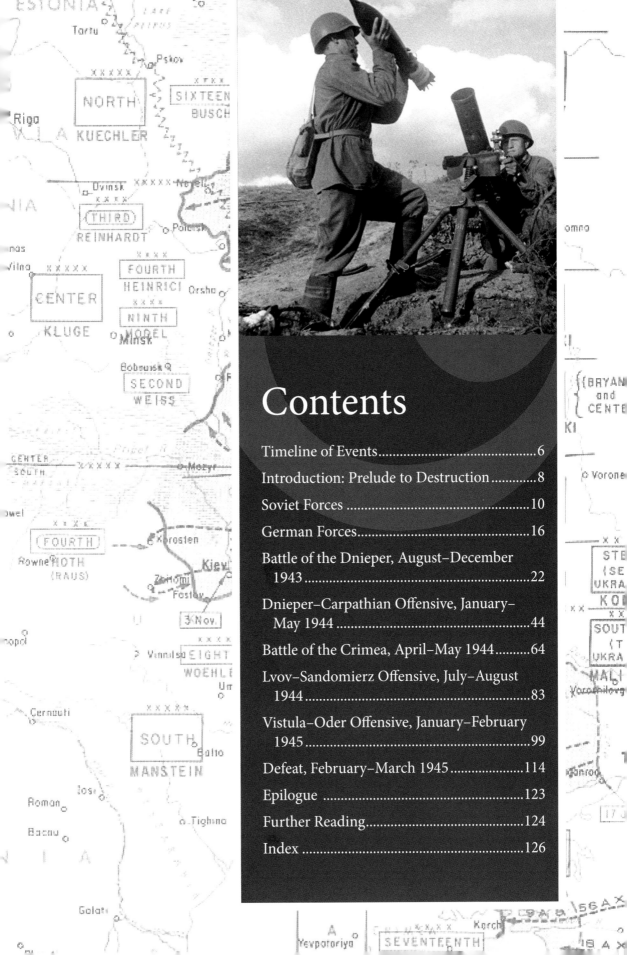

Contents

Timeline of Events

August 1943: German Army Group South begins retreating to the Dnieper River. German infantry together with their Axis allies, supported by armored units, are required to withdraw to the west bank of the river and set up a defense.

August–September 1943: German defense of the west bank of Dnieper River begins. The river line is heavily fortified, but is far from adequate to hold back the Red Army.

September 1943: Some 4,000,000 Red Army troops, stretching along an 870-mile front, advance toward the Dnieper River, and recover all territory east of the river, in one of the largest operations of World War II.

October 20, 1943: In order to liberate the Ukraine, the Soviets begin redesignating their armies in the south. Central Front is redesignated Belorussian Front, Voronezh Front is redesignated 1st Ukrainian Front, Steppe Front is redesignated 2nd Ukrainian Front, Southwestern Front is redesignated 3rd Ukrainian Front, and Southern Front is redesignated 4th Ukrainian Front.

December 24, 1943–February 29, 1944: The first phase of the Dnieper–Carpathian Offensive is launched, comprising the Zhytomyr–Berdichev Offensive (December 24, 1943–January 14, 1944), the Kirovograd Offensive (January 5–16, 1944), the Korsun–Shevchenkosky Offensive January 24–February 17, 1944), the Rovno–Lutsk Offensive (January 27–February 11, 1944), and the Nikopol–Krivoi Rog Offensive (January 30–February 29, 1944).

March 4–April 14, 1944: The second phase of the Dnieper–Carpathian Offensive begins, comprising the Proskurov–Chernovtsy Offensive (March 4–April 17), the Uman–Botosani Offensive (March 5–April 17), the Bereznegovatoye–Snigirevka Offensive (March 6–18), the Polesskoe Offensive (April 5–15), and the Odessa Offensive (March 26–April 14).

April 8, 1944: The Red Army—4th Ukrainian Front, 2nd Guards, and 51st Armies—launches the battle of the Crimea with an assault across the Perekop Isthmus.

A Sturmgeschütz III halted along the Ukrainian front, early autumn 1944. (Michael Cremin)

T-34 tanks with Soviet troops on board liberate a Ukrainian village much to the delight of the locals.

April 16, 1944: The German Seventeenth Army retreats toward Sevastopol and within a week begins the defense of the city. Some troops are evacuated by sea.

July 13, 1944: The Red Army launches the Lvov–Sandomierz Offensive to force Axis troops from Ukraine and Eastern Poland.

July 14, August 29, 1944: The 1st Ukrainian Front Lvov–Sandomierz Offensive proves an overwhelming success with three operations: the Lvov Offensive, the Stanislaw Offensive (July 13–27), and the Sandomierz Offensive (July 28–August 29).

September 1944: The Germans are expelled from the Ukraine and conduct a defense along the Vistula River. However, the Wehrmacht is unable to contain the overwhelming strength of the Red Army which penetrates the German front in southeast Poland, creating several major bridgeheads.

October 15, 1944: The 4th Ukrainian Front advances through the Carpathians on a front from the Tartar Pass to the Lupkov, and then into Ruthenia and westward into Slovakia

January 12, 1945: The 1st Belorussian Front and the 1st Ukrainian Front launch the Vistula–Oder Offensive against German Army Group A. The Soviet Fronts have a total of 163 divisions, comprising 2,203,000 infantry and 4,529 tanks. In two weeks the Soviets advance 300 miles from the Vistula to the Oder.

January 31, 1945: The Soviet offensive pauses at the Oder River whilst the 1st Belorussian, 2nd Belorussian, and 1st Ukrainian Fronts prepare for a major assault toward Berlin. At the same time, mopping-up operations clear all remaining Germans east of the Oder.

February–March 1945: The 1st Ukrainian Front participates in the Silesian and Prague operations, and the siege of Breslau. It also heavily involved in mopping-up operations outside Berlin and the battle of the Reich capital itself.

Introduction:
Prelude to Destruction

When the German invasion of Russia was launched on June 22, 1941, codenamed Operation *Barbarossa*, the German war machine divided its forces in to three army groups: North under Field Marshal Ritter von Leeb; Center under Field Marshal Fedor von Bock; and South under Field Marshal Gerd von Rundstedt. They had three objectives: Leningrad, Moscow, and the Ukraine.

In the south Rundstedt boasted the Sixth Army, Seventh Army, Eleventh Army, Romanian Fourth Army, Romanian Army Group Antonescu, and Panzergruppe 1, along with a mix of Hungarian, Italian, and Slovak units. The main thrust on the southern front was directed between the southern edge of the Pripet Marshes and the foothills of the Carpathian Mountains, with the primary objective of capturing the Ukraine. Over the coming days and weeks Germans forces made astonishing progress towards the Dnieper River despite being continually harassed by determined enemy resistance coupled with the Soviets' scorched-earth policy. But, again and again, the Soviets were overwhelmed by the rapid German onslaught.

By August 1941, the Sixth Army had swung out east of Kiev as German forces began mopping up the remnants in and around the besieged city. When the battle of Kiev finally ended on September 21, almost 665,000 Russian troops had been captured in the encirclement. Exhilarated, the Wehrmacht mercilessly pushed east, leaving a trail of devastation in its wake. Across the whole of the Sixth Army front, tanks and supporting infantry probed deeper, while the guns of the infantry divisions lengthened their range. Yet, in spite of the success of the advance through the Ukraine, most army units were not mechanized. The Sixth and Seventh Armies between them consisted of 25,000 draft horses. Although this type of transportation did not cause its commanders initial concern, by the time the army arrived at the higher Donets River in October, the weather began to change. Cold, driving rain fell and within hours the countryside was turned into a quagmire, with roads and fields virtually impassable. Many of the roads leading west from Kiev, toward Poltava and Kharkov, were now boggy swamps. Although tanks and other tracked vehicles managed to slowly negotiate the mire, animal draft, trucks, and other wheeled vehicles got hopelessly bogged down.

To make matters worse, during November, the German supply lines through Ukraine had become increasingly overstretched; vehicles were breaking down and casualties were mounting. Supply lines via rail from Lvov (also Lwow, now Lviv) to Cherkassy were also hampered by bad weather and stiff resistance. As the situation deteriorated further in northeastern Ukraine, Rundstedt, against Hitler's orders, ordered Kleist's First Panzer Army to evacuate Rostov and fall back to the Mius River, some 60 miles west of the city. On the night of November 30, Rundstedt was relieved of his command and replaced by Reichenau, a proficient but fastidious general who lacked decisiveness, and regarded Hitler as a flawless military expert.

From his command post Reichenau directed his first battle as commander of Army Group South, along the Dnieper River south of Cherkassy, to the east bank at Nikopol. It was here in freezing temperatures that Army Group South stopped the Soviet counterattack and brought the winter offensive in the southern sector to a grinding halt. Both sides were totally exhausted following weeks of ceaseless fighting.

For five months the German lines were quiet until the Soviets unleashed a spring attack at Volchansk in early May 1942 The main strike came three days later when 640,000 troops and 1,200 tanks from Timoshenko's Ukrainian Army attacked the Sixth Army and hurled it back toward Kharkov. By May 15, the Red Army threatened to envelop the city from the north and south. For two days the battered Sixth Army was subjected to incessant attack until the First Panzer and Seventeenth Armies were able to relieve the pressure. On May 20 the Germans launched a counterattack east of Kharkov and within a few days successfully linked up with Kleist west of the city, and in turn encircled the Soviets.

Simultaneously, in the Crimea the Germans were making equally good progress. Manstein's Eleventh Army launched a counterattack aimed at expelling the Soviets from the Kerch area, and resuming the offensive against Sevastopol. Opposing the Germans were 17 infantry divisions and several independent brigades. The Germans had seven infantry divisions and a panzer division. Approximately a third of the German force was Romanian. After a number of attacks in the north, the Eleventh Army broke through, driving south and pursuing the enemy to the Kerch Straits. Ten days later, on May 18, 170,000 Red Army troops surrendered.

Manstein was determined more than ever to capture the besieged city of Sevastopol. On May 21 the Germans launched a massive bombardment against Sevastopol, and for several weeks heavy artillery and aircraft attacks pounded Soviet defenses. The fortress finally fell on July 3. Two more Soviet armies had been obliterated and 90,000 prisoners taken. Hitler, elated at hearing the good news, phoned Manstein and commended him as "The Conqueror of Sevastopol," informing him that he was now a general field marshal.

Following the fall of Sevastopol and eventually the caves that dotted the peninsula, the Ukraine was almost entirely under German control. Yet, the German triumph was short-lived. Farther southeast along the Volga River, the Sixth Army was perilously embroiled at Stalingrad. By the end of 1942, the army was encircled but held out until the end of January 1943 when it finally surrendered. What followed was a dramatic reversal of fortune for the Wehrmacht in the south. Much of the German front simply collapsed as the Red Army's Central Front turned its attention west, expanding its offensive against Army Group South and Army Group Center.

During February and March, the front shifted 200 miles west, threatening the strategically important city of Kharkov. Stiff German resistance managed to slow the Soviet drive as Manstein launched a counterattack. What followed was the third battle of Kharkov. By March 15, the Germans had recaptured the city and two days later recaptured Belgorod, creating the salient which in July 1943 would lead to the battle of Kursk. The Ukraine was now under imminent Soviet threat.

| Soviet Forces

Prior to 1943 the Red Army had fought a defensive war utilizing their artillery, antitank, and armored units. Through 1943, in particular after the battle of Stalingrad and the Kursk offensive, Soviet tactics changed to begin undertaking extensive and numerous well-executed mobile offensive operations with massed armor and infantry. Tank divisions now made up some 30 percent of overall Soviet strength; independent artillery brigades and Sturmovik aircraft supported the armored units.

By early 1944 the Soviets had mastered the art of mobile warfare. Supporting the tanks was the Soviet artillery, which contained three times as many men and twice as many guns as the mobile units. Artillery was the key to the Soviet success on the battlefield and by the latter period of the war contributed to almost half the casualties inflicted on the Germans. The remainder was caused by light infantry weapons: rifles, machine guns, grenades, and mines. By 1944 the Germans were being overwhelmed by the sheer weight of numbers, manifested in the numerous Soviet offensives where the Red Army used artillery for long periods of time to soften up and then annihilate enemy positions. Yet, Soviet artillery techniques had developed little beyond the level reached in 1917. However, using up to 20,000 guns against an enemy front, Soviet gunners could systematically destroy both the front and rear of an enemy defense in depth and then draw in the enemy tanks and assault troops. Combined with the weight in numbers, it was the overwhelming firepower that achieved many of the objectives.

This success was also attributed to the enormous amount of infantry that was employed on the Eastern Front. By 1944 the Red Army had 79 infantry armies, 48 of them on the main battle front stretching from the Baltic down to the Black Sea. These 48 armies contained 405 rifle divisions, which averaged eight divisions per army. Six tank armies, which contained some rifle divisions, were mainly composed of tank and mechanized corps. The strength of the infantry armies varied in sized anywhere between 60,000 and 120,000 troops. For the offensives undertaken in the Ukraine the armies' rifle divisions would normally be brought up to strength while artillery units and independent tank and assault gun brigades would be temporarily attached.

The tank armies were often smaller, and roughly equal in strength to a typical well-supplied and up-to-strength German panzer corps. They consisted of three or four tank and mechanized corps plus a brigade or two of antitank guns and three or four artillery brigades. Attached to these corps would be combat support troops averaging between 40,000 to 65,000 men plus 700 to 1,050 armored fighting vehicles. Frequently artillery and infantry might be added to the tank army to give it more firepower.

Before the end of December 1944, German army intelligence reported that 225 Soviet infantry divisions and 22 armored corps had been identified along the Eastern Front between the Baltic and the Carpathians, assembled to attack.

This was a massive assemblage. The basic organization of the Red Army comprised two to four corps in each army. Also attached to each army were artillery and tank units as well as various service units. An artillery corps contained two or more artillery divisions as well as three or more artillery brigades. Some antiaircraft artillery corps were also organized in the Soviet order of battle. One unique corps not found in any other army during the war was a cavalry corps, generally a division-sized force of mounted infantry supported by light artillery and tanks.

The tanks were the backbone of the offensive. Each tank corps comprised some 10,500 men and 189 tanks, and each mechanized corps 16,000 men and 186 tanks. Following in close support of the tanks were the rifle divisions which were primarily made up of combat troops with a small logistical component. The Soviets also formed Guards rifle corps, which were often assigned control of regular rifle divisions (and at times controlled no Guards rifle divisions). A typical rifle division totaled 9,375 troops; a Guards rifle division 10,585 troops. A rifle corps consisted of two to three rifle divisions, and about three corps made up a Soviet army, known by the Soviets as a 'Front'.

In Profile:
Soviet Commanders, 1943–45

Belorussian Front, October 20, 1943–February 17, 1944

Originally this was the Central Front, which on October 20, 1943, was redesignated as the Belorussian Front, and then the 1st Belorussian Front on February 17, 1944.

GENERAL KONSTANTIN KONSTANTINOVICH ROKOSSOVSKY

The Belorussian Front was placed under the command of General Rokossovsky who had commanded the Central Front up to October 1943. He was a very capable leader, but was

often too independent-minded and difficult to direct. However, he had performed brilliantly on the battlefield and had played major roles in the battles at Moscow, Stalingrad, and Kursk. Following these, his reputation was assured and he was given the task of driving the Belorussian Front into the Ukraine. Following the Dnieper–Carpathian Offensive, the Belorussian Front was renamed the 1st Belorussian Front on February 17, 1944. Through 1944, Rokossovsky conducted a number of brilliant tactical offensives against the Wehrmacht. Out in the field in front of his commanders he showed great nerve, determination, and strength, and was a man of his word. His success saw him being transferred in November 1944 to the 2nd Belorussian Front, in time to direct two major offensives in the Baltic states.

1st Belorussian Front, November 1944–May 1945

MARSHAL GEORGY KONSTANTINOVICH ZHUKOV

Following Rokossovsky's transfer to the Baltics, Marshal Zhukov was appointed commander of 1BF, in November 1944, for its last two great offensives of the war. Zhukov was a brilliant

tactical commander. He had organized the defense of Leningrad before appointment as commander-in-chief of the western front. He directed the defense of Moscow as well as the massive counteroffensive that drove the German Army Group Center back from central Russia in late 1941. He became the chief member of Joseph Stalin's personal supreme headquarters and figured significantly in the planning and implementation of almost every major engagement in the war. He oversaw major offensive and defensive actions and planned and directed the counteroffensive that encircled the German Sixth Army at Stalingrad. He was named a Marshal of the Soviet Union soon afterward. Zhukov was heavily involved in the planning for the battle of Kursk and masterminded the Soviet advance across Ukraine in the winter of 1943/4 and spring of 1944. He was an exceptional leader and a superb tactician. Out on the battlefield in front of his men he showed boldness and a readiness to accept risks and challenges.

1st Ukrainian Front, October 20, 1943–May 1945

GENERAL NIKOLAI VATUTIN

On October 20, 1943, the Voronezh Front was renamed the 1st Ukrainian Front. Soviet

command changed the name to replicate the westward advance of the Red Army during operations in the Ukraine against German Army Group South.

General Vatutin was given the command of the 1st Ukrainian Front in October 1943. As a commander he had a clear and compelling view of strategy and logistics and a sound and balanced touch for grand operations. He was responsible for many Red Army operations in the Ukraine as commander of the Southwestern Front and the Voronezh Front during the battle of Kursk. Although he was often at a military disadvantage, including resources inferior to those of his enemy, he was brilliantly successful in attack and remarkably resourceful in defense.

However, his command would be short-lived. On February 28, 1944 whilst planning a new operation on the way to Slavuta, Vatutin was ambushed by Ukrainian insurgents far behind the front lines near the village of Mylyatyn. He was rushed to hospital in Kiev but died of sepsis six weeks later. Vatutin was given a state funeral in Kiev. He was succeeded by Georgy Zhukov.

MARSHAL GEORGY KONSTANTINOVICH ZHUKOV

Following Vatutin's untimely death, Marshal Zhukov was given command of the 1st Ukrainian Front in March 1944, which saw him taking charge of the planning of the Dnieper–Carpathian Offensive against German Army Group South and elements of Army Group Center. The strategic offensive was key to the Red Army gaining significant ground in the Ukraine and which subsequently saw the destruction of some 20 Wehrmacht divisions. In spite of inhospitable terrain, vast distances, inadequate rations for his troops, and shortages of fuel, he produced the unexpected. Directing his forces during the offensive enlarged his outlook from a tactical view to one of strategic scope. Following this successful offensive, in May 1944, Zhukov was sent to the central area of the front to prepare and coordinate the 1st Belorussian and 2nd Belorussian Fronts for the Soviet summer offensive known as Operation *Bagration*.

MARSHAL IVAN S. KONEV

In May 1944, Marshal Konev took command of the 1st Ukrainian Front, which had seen considerable success in the Dnieper–Carpathian Offensive. As a commander he was admired by his troops, not merely for his inspirational leadership, but as a superb strategist. He was the first general to lead the first real counterattack of the war on the Eastern Front. Using surprise and deception, he stopped German tank supremo General Heinz Guderian's advance on Moscow by employing what became known as the "Konev ambush"—a planned retreat of troops in the center, with the flanks then snapping shut across the breach to trap the pursuing enemy. This was a grand masterplan which he employed throughout the war. When he became commander of the 2nd Ukrainian Front in July 1943, he distinguished himself at the battle of Kursk again using deception as the key to his success. Konev was made a Marshal of the Soviet Union in March 1944. In August 1944, his 1st Ukrainian Front was the first to carry the fighting beyond Soviet frontiers, advancing through Poland and across the Vistula River. His troops were the first on German soil and reached the Oder where he linked up with Zhukov's forces before the planned assault against Berlin.

2nd Ukrainian Front, October 20, 1943–May 29, 1945

On October 20, 1943 the Steppe Front was renamed the 2nd Ukrainian Front.

GENERAL RODION MALINOVSKY

General Malinovsky was a brilliant tactical commander both in offensive and defensive operations. In February 1943, he resumed his command of the Southern Front, and in less than two weeks he had expelled Manstein's forces from Rostov-on-Don, opening the road to the Ukraine for the Red Army. Following his successful command of the 3rd Ukrainian Front, he was given the command of the 2nd Ukrainian Front in May 1944. His sole objective was to force the Germans out of remaining Soviet territory. He took over the final stages of the Jassy–Kishinve Offensive, a coordinated attack against Romania aimed at splitting the enemy in the Ukraine and retreating German units. On September 10, 1944, Malinovsky was recalled to Moscow, and made a Marshal of the Soviet Union. Later that month he was back on the battlefield continuing his offensive drive and crossing into Hungary. His strategic and operational skills enabled him to overcome his troops' weaknesses and to successfully conquer Budapest on February 13, 1945.

3rd Ukrainian Front, October 20, 1943–May 29, 1945

After October 20, 1943 the Southwestern Front was renamed the 3rd Ukrainian Front.

GENERAL RODION MALINOVSKY

When the Southwestern Front was renamed 3rd Ukrainian Front in October 1943, General Malinovsky became commander. He was tasked with attacking the Panther–Wotan Line, and securing the bridgeheads on the eastern banks of the Dnieper. As a commander he was highly admired by his men and by Stalin himself, not just for his charisma, but for his masterly strategy in modern warfare. A brilliant general, Malinovsky was courageous, zealous, a master of surprise and a risk-taker. His success against German Army Group South saw him lead his men in isolating German forces in the Crimea. In May 1944, Malinovsky was transferred to the 2nd Ukrainian Front.

MARSHAL FYODOR TOLBUKHIN

General Tolbukhin was transferred to take control of the 3rd Ukrainian Front in May 1944. As a brilliant tactical commander, he quickly got to work to plan his summer campaign, launching an invasion of the Balkans, whilst the remainder of the Soviet forces in the south continued fighting in the Ukraine. Tolbukin went on to liberate Bulgaria and then marched into Yugoslavia before invading southern Hungary.

4th Ukrainian Front, October 20, 1943–May 1945

The front was first formed on 20 October 20, 1943, by renaming the Southern Front which was operating on the Lower Dnieper and in the Crimea. After the liberation of the Crimea the front was disbanded in May 1944. However, in August 1944, it was created for the second time by separating the left wing of the 1st Ukrainian Front.

GENERAL FYODOR TOLBUKHIN

In October 1943, General Tolbukhin was transferred to the 4th Ukrainian Front. Tolbukhin assisted Rodion Malinovsky's 3rd Ukrainian Front during operations in the Lower Dnieper Offensive and the Dnieper–Carpathian Offensive. As a commander he was liked by his men and was one of few Soviet generals who was trusted by Stalin. On the battlefield he was stern-faced, so typical of Soviet commanders, but he was approachable. In front of his enemy, he had the ability to adapt rapidly to constantly changing conditions on the field of battle. He was both master of defense and offense. In May 1944, he was transferred to the 3rd Ukrainian Front.

GENERAL IVAN YEFIMOVICH PETROV

For the second time the 4th Ukrainian Front was created on August 4, 1944, by separating the left wing of the 1st Ukrainian Front. Commanding the 4th Ukrainian Front was General Petrov. He led his soldiers successfully and planned the Carpathian Offensive simultaneously with the battle of the Dukla Pass. He then moved his front toward central Slovakia, as well as unleashing the Moravian–Ostrava Offensive on the Polish–Moravian border. This culminated in the Prague Offensive, the last battle in which he would lead his men until, in March 1945, he became Chief of Staff 1st Ukrainian Front.

GENERAL ANDREY IVANOVICH YERYOMENKO

On March 26, 1945, General Yeryomenko was transferred from the 2nd Baltic Front to command the 4th Ukrainian Front until the end of the war. Yeryomenko's front was positioned in eastern Hungary where the subsequent offensive helped capture the rest of Hungary, and pave the way for the Soviet liberation of Czechoslovakia. His army liberated many towns and cities in Czechoslovakia. Today, several streets in the Czech Republic still bear his name.

| German Forces

Prior to 1943 the German Wehrmacht had fought a war in the Soviet Union that was mainly on the offensive. The troops that entered Russia were well trained, well supplied and armed with ample modern weaponry. However, it severely lacked vehicles: one of the biggest flaws in the German arsenal was that it was not fully motorized and relied heavily on animal draught to tow supplies and artillery.

In response to the war in Russia and with the prospect of fighting a protracted war, the Germans actually confiscated some 290,000 vehicles from occupied countries to increase fleet numbers. Even so, by the end of 1943, the German lack of motorization was having a noticeable effect on its operations. Having gone over to the defensive, the non-motorized infantry often could no longer rapidly withdraw from one part of the front to another. Instead, units found themselves trapped and destroyed. In the Ukraine, the few German mobile divisions that were available had to spend days and sometimes weeks propping up the receding front. When infantry were ordered to withdraw to another line of defense, tank units had to support and cover non-motorized units as they slowly deployed to another position. This sometimes came at a great price to the panzer crews.

Infantry played a crucial part in maintaining the disintegrating front. The superior efficiency and mobility of the German soldier had been a critical factor in the German success. However, by January 1944, casualties were so great that replacing them was almost impossible. In southern Russia, no less than 12 entire divisions were destroyed in early 1944. By mid-year, a further 29 divisions would be annihilated. The infantry loss in numbers was bad enough, but many of these men were battle-hardened and well trained. Unable to provide front line units with adequate replacements, the remaining troops had to fight on, regardless of the losses in men and equipment. In order to try and make up some of these losses, due to the declining strength of the Luftwaffe, the front lines gained an additional 100,000 airmen, most of whom had the mammoth task of defending the skies with antiaircraft guns.

Supporting the ground troops was often left to the Panzerwaffe, the tank force. In late 1943 only five panzer divisions and one SS panzer division were deployed as replacements on the Eastern Front. Of these, only the 1st SS Panzer Division Leibstandarte and the 1st Panzer Division were at full strength, with two battalions of tanks. The 14th, 24th, and 25th Panzer Divisions comprised of a various mixture of tanks and assault guns in a single battalion. The units in the south, however, consisting of the 1st, 8th, 16th, and 17th Panzer Divisions, were only at half strength.

Yet, in spite of the lack of strength in the Panzerwaffe, the German armaments industry actually began producing a range of new vehicles in 1944, especially for operations in Army Group South. In fact, during 1944, the Panzerwaffe was better supplied with equipment than at any other time on the Eastern Front. In total, some 20,000 fighting vehicles, including 8,328 medium and heavy tanks, 5,751 assault guns, 3,617 tank destroyers, and 1,246 self-propelled artillery pieces of various types reached the Eastern Front. Included in these new arrivals were the second generation of tank destroyers, the Jagdpanzer IV, followed by the Hetzer and then the Jagpanther and Jagdtiger. During 1944, tank destroyers and assault guns would soon outnumber tanks, which was confirmation of the Panzerwaffe's obligation of performing a defensive role against overwhelming opposition.

All of these vehicles would be irrevocably stretched along a very thin Eastern Front, with many of them rarely reaching proper operating levels. Panzer divisions too were often broken up and split among hastily thrown-together battle groups, or *Kampfgruppen*, drawn from assorted armored formations. Even still, these *Kampfgruppen* were put into the line well below nominal strength. The demands put on the Panzerwaffe during 1944 were immeasurable. The constant employment, coupled with the nightmare of not having enough supplies, was a worry that perpetually festered in the minds of commanders. The Red Army, encouraged by the Germans' dire situation, was now mounting bolder operations aimed directly against the German front. With infantry losses mounting, it was left to the Panzerwaffe to hold the lines, which in turn saw their rapid reduction in strength by the end of the year.

The armored panzer divisions totaled 14,750 troops with some 160 tanks. A division was organized into an armored regiment with two tank battalions and two infantry regiments, each with two battalions, along with a variety of supporting units which included reconnaissance, engineers, and signals. In addition to its panzers, the division was armed with 77 guns ranging from 7.5cm to 15cm, 133 PaK guns, 70 mortars, and 700 machine guns.

As for German motorized infantry divisions or panzergrenadier divisions, those elements not reliant on animal draught, also contained 14,750 men. A division was organized into two regiments, each with two battalions of infantry. These divisions were equipped with supporting units and weapons similar to those of an armored division, apart from the fact that the motorized division had no tanks. It did however have 45 assault guns.

In the Waffen-SS armored divisions, their composition was slightly different and comprised six rather than four battalions of infantry; some divisions totaled as many as 20,000 troops.

German infantry divisions nominally had nine battalions and numbered about 15,000 men, but most infantry divisions were organized into three regiments with only two battalions each. The six-battalion divisions numbered about 12,500 men. A division was armed with 24 infantry guns and howitzers comprising 7.5cm and 15cm pieces, 48 field and medium guns of 10.5cm and 150cm calibers, 76 mortars, and 650 light and heavy machine guns. For transport, the division had 615 motor vehicles and 1,450 horse-drawn vehicles.

In Profile:
German Commanders, 1943–45

Army Group South

Army Group South operated from June 22, 1941 until April 4, 1944. It was then split into two and designated Army Group North Ukraine and Army Group South Ukraine.

GENERAL FIELD MARSHAL FRITZ ERICH GEORG EDUARD VON MANSTEIN

General Field Marshal Erich von Manstein was one of the most distinguished Eastern Front generals of the war. He had superb strategic sense, combined with a great understanding of his men and the weaponry at his disposal. Outspoken, confident, and level headed, he did not fear Hitler and told him the reality of the situation on the battlefield. As a master tactician in the Soviet Union Manstein achieved great success in Southern Russia and believed that the battle of the Kursk was a kind of victory for Germany as it destroyed much of the Soviet military capacity to wage further large-scale offensives through 1943. However, as commander of Army Group South, he was totally aware of the deteriorating situation and argued incessantly with Hitler, even asking to resign his post. However, as further setbacks continued in the south, the Führer finally conceded and the field marshal was sacked at the end of March 1944. He was replaced by General Field Marshal Walter Model. (Bundesarchiv Bild 183-H01758)

Army Group North Ukraine

On April 4, 1944, Army Group South was redesignated Army Group North Ukraine. Army Group North Ukraine existed from April 4 to September 28, 1944.

GENERAL FIELD MARSHAL OTTO MORITZ WALTER MODEL

Field Marshal Model's replacement of Manstein was, as Hitler outlined, to instill new vigor and restore determination into Army Group South which was renamed Army Group North Ukraine. Model had been a very successful Eastern Front commander and his ability to adapt to constantly changing conditions on the battlefield, earned him much respect among his men. He was a master of defense whom Hitler came to rely on as his "troubleshooter" or "firefighter." His ingenuity enabled him to salvage apparently hopeless situations and hold the line at all costs. Although he had a paradoxical personality, he had the absolute trust of those who fought for him, not mention the Führer. Out on the battlefield in front of his men Model was energetic, courageous, innovative,

and friendly with his enlisted men. As commander of Army Group South, he was given the mammoth task of trying to mitigate the disaster on the west bank of the Dnieper. However, even Model, who was above all a realist, could not avoid the deepening crisis in the Ukraine. When the Red Army finally took the initiative in the East against Army Group Center in June 1944, the German front buckled and Hitler quickly called for Model's assistance, calling on him to take over the center.

Army Group South Ukraine

Army Group South Ukraine was created on April 5, 1944 by renaming Army Group A.

GENERAL FIELD MARSHAL FERDINAND SCHÖRNER

In March 1944 General Field Marshal Schörner was made commander of Army Group A. Within two months he was promoted to command Army Group South Ukraine following General Field Marshal Model's quick departure to help prop up the decimated Army Group Center front. As a general, Schörner was regarded as a brutal leader. He dealt with his men harshly and looked upon the Russian race as subhuman. Yet, in spite of his racist, often arrogant, and distasteful tendencies, he was regarded as an excellent defensive tactician. When he took over command of Army Group South Ukraine his troops were in headlong retreat. He quickly put together a slow tactical withdrawal to save his army group from complete disaster in the Ukraine. In the Crimea, his methods of defense had little effect in spite of his ordering a "scorched earth" policy. The military situation was made worse in the south with most of the reinforcements being sent to plug gaps in Army Group Center and Army Group North. The commander of Army Group North, General Johannes Friessner, argued incessantly with Hitler over freedom of withdrawal. In the Führer's eyes, the situation demanded a fierce defensive tactician in the north. It was decided that Friessner and Schörner would exchange commands. Friessner got the worst of the swap. (Bundesarchiv Bild 183-L22898)

GENERAL JOHANNES FRIESSNER

General Friessner was an exceptional commander, accessible and popular among his men. He was no automaton and could be very independent-minded. He detested rule-breaking and insubordination, and demanded openness and honesty of his men. However, in spite of his appointment as commander of Army Group South Ukraine, his position was already doomed, and circumstances on battlefield meant that whatever he did, his days were numbered. Unable to halt the four-month Soviet offensive by Marshal Rodion Malinovsky's 2nd Ukrainian Front, Friessner continually argued with Hitler about withdrawing his army group. As far as the Führer was concerned, the general had clearly failed as a commander. On December 22, 1944, he was relieved of his command.

Army Group A

Army Group A was formed a third time, on September 23, 1944, in the southern areas of Poland and the Carpathians by renaming Army Group North Ukraine.

GENERAL FIELD MARSHAL PAUL LUDWIG EWALD VON KLEIST

General von Kleist took command of Army Group A on November 22, 1942. During his service as commander, he proved to be an extremely capable leader in a precarious and dangerous situation. As a person Kleist was outspoken, determined, and blunt. He also valued morals on the battlefield and had a humane policy in regards to his enemy. However, his job on the southern front was difficult and plagued with military setbacks and problems. In spite of numerous orders from Hitler to prevent the withdrawal of his forces, he often ignored the requests, to save his men from annihilation. But Kleist's command continued to be problematic, characterized by increasing friction with Hitler over the Führer's handling of the war in the East. Both men argued continuously, with Kleist calling for the abandonment of certain areas of the Ukraine including the Crimea, whilst Hitler demanded the troops stand firm and fight to the last. In their last meeting, the general took the opportunity to urge his Führer to make peace with Stalin while he had time. Hitler curtly replied that it would never happen. Kleist was then sacked along with Manstein on March 30, 1944. (Bundesarchiv Bild 183-1986-0210-503)

GENERAL JOSEF HARPE

From August 16 until September 23, 1944 General Josef Harpe took command of Army Group North Ukraine until it was redesignated Army Group A for the third time. Harpe was a prototype Prussian officer of the old school. He was blindly obedient and held a high moral code on the battlefield. Taking command of an army group was not an easy task and the war situation coupled with massive losses made him very nervous. By 1945 the condition of his men had deteriorated to the extent of him committing his last reserves and sending service personnel into combat as ad hoc formations. Nevertheless, the Red Army continued gaining ground, in spite of orders from Hitler to hold the line. In mid-January 1945 Harpe was finally relieved of his command and blamed by Hitler for his inability to stop the Soviet Vistula–Oder Offensive, which resulted in the Soviet capture of most of Poland. (Bundesarchiv Bild 146-1981-104-30)

GENERAL FIELD MARSHAL FERDINAND SCHÖRNER

From March 25 to March 31, 1944 General Schörner took command of Army Group A. It was a temporary position as the army group was redesignated as Army Group South Ukraine on April 5.

Army Group South, December 1944–April 1945

In September 1944, Army Group South Ukraine was redesignated Army Group South.

GENERAL OTTO WÖHLER

In December 1944, General Wöhler was appointed commander of Army Group South. By the time he took command, its forces were already in full retreat and falling back onto a number of defensive lines. As a commander Wöhler was a strict disciplinarian and brutal on the battlefield. In fact, earlier on the Eastern Front, whilst serving as Chief of Staff of the Eleventh Army he cooperated with the Special Action Groups or *Einsatzgruppen* who roamed behind the front lines murdering Jews and others regarded as non-desirable to the Nazi regime. Hitler looked upon Wöhler as a commander who would instill fanaticism into his troops and encourage them to fight to the death. However, the military situation by this late period of the war was hopeless, despite his excessive optimism that often clouded his judgement. As the front began to completely collapse on April 2, 1945, the remnants of Army Group South were redesignated as Army Group Ostmark. By this time, Wöhler had completely lost his grip of the situation. He was sacked on April 6, 1945 without issuing any orders to Army Group Ostmark. (Bundesarchiv Bild 183-2007-0313-500)

Army Group Ostmark, April 2–May 8, 1945

Army Group Ostmark was formed on April 2, 1945 from the remnants of Army Group South.

GENERAL DR. LOTHAR RENDULIC

General Rendulic was the only commander during the 36-day existence of this army group. The formation was thrown together for defensive operations in Austria and the Protectorate of Bohemia and Moravia. He was a distinguished Eastern Front commander and appealed to Hitler for his brutal conduct on the battlefield and his hatred of the enemy. He believed in indiscriminately terrorizing the population, murdering civilians, and wholeheartedly supporting the scorched earth policy. However, not even his fierce conduct could prevent the inevitable collapse of the front. On May 7, 1945, following the Soviet Prague offensive, Rendulic reluctantly surrendered Army Group Ostmark to the 71st Infantry Division of the U.S Army in Austria. (Bundesarchiv Bild 146-1995-027-32A)

Battle of the Dnieper, August–December 1943

The defeat of the German Panzerwaffe at Kursk in July 1943 was so devastating to the German war machine on the Eastern Front that it unquestionably led to their forces taking their first steps of retreat back toward the Reich. The Soviets had managed to destroy no less than 30 divisions, seven of which were panzer divisions. German reinforcements were insufficient to replace the staggering losses, so the Panzerwaffe fought on understrength.

The reverberations caused by the defeat at Kursk meant that German forces in Army Group South bore the brunt of the heaviest Soviet drive. Both the Soviet Voronezh and Steppe Fronts possessed massive local superiority against anything the Germans had on the battlefield, and this included their diminishing resources of tanks and assault guns. The Wehrmacht was now dutybound to improvise with what they had at their disposal and try to maintain themselves in the field. However, it was in the south where the weight of the Soviet effort was now directed, during the second half of 1943. Stiff defensive action was now the stratagem, but the Germans lacked sufficient reinforcements and the strength of their armored units dwindled steadily as they tried to hold back the Soviet might.

During the first uneasy weeks of August 1943 the First Panzer Army and Armeeabteilung Kempf (army detachment) fought to hold ground along the Donets River whilst the final

A Schwimmwagen crosses the Dnieper River during a unit's withdrawal to the west bank in the summer of 1943.

22

battle of Kharkov played out. Farther north near the battered town of Akhtyrka the Fourth Panzer Army was also fighting a frenzied battle of attrition. Along the whole front massive Soviet artillery bombardments swept the German lines and inflicted considerable casualties. Throughout August and September German infantry and armored units tried frantically to hold the receding front. With just over 1,000 panzers operating in Southern Russia the Germans were seriously understrength, further depleted by vehicles being constantly taken out of action for repair. Along many areas of the front, high losses resulted from inadequate supplies, and not from the skill of the attackers.

By October 1943, both Army Group Center and Army Group South had been pushed back an average distance of 150 miles across a 650-mile front. Despite heavy resistance in many sectors of the front the Soviets lost no time in regaining as much territory as possible. In Army Group South where the front threatened to completely collapse under intense enemy pressure, frantic appeals to Hitler were made by commander of Army Group South, Field Marshal Manstein, to withdraw his forces across the Dnieper River. What followed was a fighting withdrawal that degenerated into a race with the Soviets for possession of the river. As German units fell back, the fighting was ferocious which saw Heer and Waffen-SS troops fanatically contesting every town and city.

The Heer made extensive use of employing rearguard units, leaving troops in each city and on each hill to slow the Soviet offensive. As the bulk of Army Group South withdrew, panzer divisions covered the rear with columns pulling back to selected river crossing points at Cherkassy, Dniepropetrovsk, Kiev, Kanev, and Krmenchug, leaving behind a charred wasteland.

The crossing of the Dnieper River, before the battered front disintegrated into total ruin, was one of Manstein's major achievements. The Germans still believed they could

A Soviet 57mm M1943 or ZiS-2 antitank gun during a fire mission along the Dnieper. These weapons were employed by antitank artillery platoons of infantry units and antitank artillery regiments.

Soviet riflemen march toward the Dnieper using the edge of a field along a muddy road as cover.

stabilize the front, but Soviet numerical superiority was far too great. By trying to hold the eastern side of the Dnieper the Germans had sapped most of the strength from Army Group South and Army Group Center. German infantrymen, together with their Axis allies and supported by armored units, were now required to try and perform yet another reversal of Germany's misfortunes in the East. German doctrine along the Dnieper was no longer to adopt any risky offensives but to use a delaying and blocking strategy instead.

By the summer of 1943 the Red Army on the German southern front had become more mobile, whilst the Germans struggled to maintain any type of cohesion. Soviet infantry units managed to keep the Germans on the run by heavily reinforcing their troops

A column of T-34/85 tanks advance, supported by motorcycle combinations. Note the assault troops riding on the tanks. Once the tank got to the forward edge of the battlefield the soldiers would dismount and go into action.

A Soviet 76mm 3-K air defense gun M1938 being prepared along the Dnieper.

The ubiquitous 76mm divisional gun M1942 or ZiS-3 during a fire mission.

with armored units usually comprising tanks and a regiment of self-propelled guns. In addition, they could draw on at least two powerful brigades of artillery and four engineer battalions. All this was used to maximum effect against growing and fortified German positions.

By August 1943 the strength of the Red Army and its systematic use of long-range intensive bombardments and massed infantry and armor assaults gradually pushed back both Heer and Waffen-SS units of Army Group South. As the German forces withdrew toward the Dnieper River a scorched earth policy was implemented, stripping the areas they had abandoned of anything of use to the Soviet war effort.

As the Germans crossed to the west bank of the river, on September 15, Hitler ordered Army Group South to immediately draw up plans to fortify the river line against Soviet attacks. The Dnieper was to be used as a natural barrier against the Soviets; every soldier on the front line was required to conduct an effective, almost fanatical, resistance in the face of overwhelming enemy strength and build a series of fortified defenses. These defenses were manned along the banks of the river and also set back in special defensive positions—belts—comprising antitank strongpoints, and an extensive network of engineer obstacles. The strength of the German defenses varied considerably. Where it was expected that the Soviets would attack, German commanders tried to concentrate the largest number of defenders on the narrowest frontages. In general, the Germans were able to build a number of defensive belts that extended in depth for miles. Although these belts in places consisted of nothing more than lines of trenches with various tank obstacles, other sectors of the front were turned into impressive strongholds which included dozens of reinforced machine-gun and mortar pits. Each line of defense was heavily mined and consisted of antitank strongpoints

A Soviet artillery column bound for the front in the summer of 1943. Artillery regiments comprised three basic types of guns: howitzers, heavy mortars, and rocket launchers.

and a network of obstacles protected by extensive barbed-wire barriers. Manning these lines were well-dug-in troops armed with an assortment of weapons. Antitank obstacles and lines of trenches, where possible, supported an assortment of antitank and artillery guns. The principal antitank weapon was the 7.5cm PaK 40. On average some 24 were supplied to each division, which often helped supplement the diminishing numbers of 8.8cm antiaircraft guns.

Two of the main weapons used in both offensive and defensive roles were the MG 34 and MG 42 machine guns. With a good field of fire and sufficient ammunition, an MG crew could hold up Soviet infantry on a one-mile front. Normally the Germans would have 32 to 65 machine guns per mile of front. Just one of these machine guns that survived the preparatory Soviet bombardment could stall an entire enemy advance.

However, in spite of areas where the Dnieper line was heavily fortified, it was far from adequate to hold back the Red Army. Like many parts of the front, the Germans were overstretched, underarmed, and undermanned. Consequently, troops were compelled to defend their positions to the grim death, knowing that they had limited stocks of weapons and dire shortages of ammunition. The lack of armored support too was another deep concern for the German soldier which brought about considerable apprehension. Manstein himself was under no illusion as to the task ahead. He was fully aware his forces were dwarfed by Soviet numerical superiority and that he would not be able to contain his enemy for any appreciable length of time. In desperation, he requested 12 new divisions in the hope of at least temporarily containing the Soviet offensive.

German troops dug in along the banks of the Dnieper. Note the MG 42 machine gun overlooking the river. This gun and how it was positioned would have caused significant losses to any assaulting troops attempting to cross the river.

A Soviet map of the battle of the Dnieper. The red arrows indicate the Red Army advance from the Dnieper into Western Ukraine.

In Profile:
Volkswagen Schwimmwagen & SU-122 Self-propelled Howitzer

Volkswagen Schwimmwagen, Dnieper River September 1943

Schwimmwagen means floating or swimming car. This amphibious four-wheel-drive off-roader was used extensively by both the Heer and Waffen-SS during operations on the Eastern Front. The Type 166 is the most numerous mass-produced amphibious car in history. (Oliver Missing)

SU-122 Self-propelled Howitzer, Dnieper River, October 1943

The SU-122 was found in medium self-propelled artillery regiments which consisted of four batteries of four SU-122s in each. Each regiment was also equipped with either an additional SU-122 or a T-34 for the commander. The SU-122 proved effective in its intended role of direct fire against strong defensive positions. (Oliver Missing)

Red Army troops during a fire mission against German targets withdrawing across the Dnieper.

It was one of the largest operations of the war on the Eastern Front involved almost three million Red Army troops that stretched along an 870-mile front. Its objective was to advance to the Dnieper River, and recover from the German forces all land east of the river. The main drive of the offensive was in a southwesterly direction. The offensive began almost a month after the battle of the Kursk, on 26 August 1943. Red Army formations began advancing on a front that stretched from Smolensk to the Sea of Azov. In total the operation would be undertaken by 36 combined arms, four tank and five air armies. Some 2,650,000 personnel were brought into the ranks for the operation that would utilize 51,000 guns and mortars, 2,400 tanks, and 2,850 aircraft.

In operations east of the Dnieper River the Red Army achieved an overwhelming superiority of forces along the front. Its courageous and relentless concentration of forces allowed many of its units to destroy some of the most formidable German positions. This powerful concentration, comprising the Belorussian, 1st, 2nd, 3rd, and 4th Ukrainian Fronts used waves of armored and infantry divisions to maintain the rapid advance.

One of the contributing factors to the Soviet advance to the Dnieper was the superiority in armor. The Soviets had allocated almost half of its available armored vehicles for close infantry support in order. These Soviet formations were often formed into mobile groups to exploit breakthroughs and penetrate the front in depth. They would then proceed at speed and encircle overwhelmed German forces in the enemy rear. These concentrations of Soviet armor in the breakthrough area were vast.

Soviet troops with a mixture of weaponry cross the Dnieper River to secure a bridgehead on the west bank.

Red Army soldiers during an amphibious assault across the Dnieper. The Soviets had little experience of large amphibious attacks. However, they were crucial to the success in securing positions on the west bank of the river.

Supporting the attacks was the Soviet artillery. Its weight and intensity were formidable. Before any major attack, Red Army artillery, Katyusha rockets, and mortar batteries would open up a storm of fire lasting up to two hours. Then, when the infantry launched their attack, they were preceded by a rolling barrage of rockets and bombs. Troops would attack toward the objective supported by advancing tanks and self-propelled vehicles as projectiles thundered over them, smashing into the German lines.

Along the entire front the Soviet artillery devoted the majority of its time to supporting ground attacks and pulverizing areas deep in the German lines. From the air too came the Red Army Air Force, which conducted thousands of sorties against enemy troop concentrations and artillery positions.

Fortunately for the Red Army assault units the Germans had been unable to complete their defenses along the river, with many parts of the line having no density and depth of fortifications. The Soviets took advantage of this and began concentrating in areas where assault crossings were most likely to be more successful, such as near Kremenchuk, Nikopol, and Zaporizhia.

Soviet troops along the east bank of the Dnieper prepare to climb into rubber boats to undertake the often-perilous river crossing.

Dead German soldiers lying in a rubber boat, killed whilst trying to escape from the east bank of the Dnieper.

Once the Soviets had secured a bridgehead along the Dnieper, pontoon bridges were immediately constructed in order to quickly move heavy armor across. In this photograph sappers are preparing a pontoon. Note the soldier anxiously looking skyward for enemy aircraft.

A U.S. Army map of the battle of the Dnieper and Red Army advances from the Dnieper into Western Ukraine. (U.S. Army)

EASTERN EUROPE, 1941

28

SOVIET SUMMER AND FALL OFFENSIVES

Operations, 17 July–1 December 1943

SCALE OF MILES

New Front Designations (in parenthesis) were effective on 20 October 1943

MERETSKOV — VOLKHOV

NORTHWEST (SECOND BALTIC) M. M. POPOV

GOVOROV — LENINGRAD

NORTH KUECHLER — EIGHTEENTH LINDEMANN — SIXTEENTH BUSCH

KALININ (FIRST BALTIC) YEREMENKO (BAGRAMYAN)

WEST SOKOLOVSKI

WHITE RUSSIAN ROKOSSOVSKI

BRYANSK and CENTER

VORONEZH (FIRST UKRAINIAN) VATUTIN

STEPPE (SECOND UKRAINIAN) KONEV

SOUTHWEST (THIRD UKRAINIAN) MALINOVSKI

SOUTH (FOURTH UKRAINIAN) TOLBUKHIN

NORTH CAUCASUS PETROV

CENTER KLUGE — THIRD REINHARDT — FOURTH HEINRICI — NINTH MODEL — SECOND WEISS

FOURTH (RAUS)

SOUTH MANSTEIN — EIGHTH WOEHLER — FIRST MACKENSEN (HUBE) — SIXTH HOLLIDT

A JAENECKE — SEVENTEENTH

BLACK SEA FLEET VLADIMIROVSKI

SWEDEN — ESTONIA — LATVIA — LITHUANIA — EAST PRUSSIA — POLAND — GERMANY — CZECHOSLOVAKIA — CARPATHIAN — AUSTRIA — HUNGARY — RUMANIA — BESSARABIA — BULGARIA — YUGOSLAVIA — BALTIC SEA — BLACK SEA

Red Army Order of Battle

CENTRAL FRONT

(Redesignated Belorussian Front from October 20, 1943)

Commander: Konstantin Rokossovsky

2nd Tank Army

9th Tank Army

13th Army

48th Army

60th Army

61st Army

70th Army

16th Air Army

VORONEZH FRONT

(Redesignated 1st Ukrainian Front from October 20, 1943)

Commander: Nikolai Vatutin

3rd Guards Tank Army

1st Tank Army

4th Guards Tank Corps

1st Guard Cavalry Corps

5th Guards Army

6th Guards Army

38th Army

47th Army

27th Army

52nd Army

2nd Air Army

STEPPE FRONT

(Redesignated 2nd Ukrainian Front from October 20, 1943)

Commander: Rodion Malinovsky

6th Guards Tank Army

4th Guards Army

7th Guards Army

27th Army

40th Army

52nd Army

53rd Army

18th Tank Corps

5th Guards Cavalry Corps

23rd Tank Corps

SOUTHWESTERN FRONT

(Redesignated 3rd Ukrainian Front from October 20, 1943)

Commander: Rodion Malinovsky

1ST GUARDS ARMY

6th Guards Rifle Corps

20th Guards Rifle Division

152nd Rifle Division

34th Rifle Corps

6th Rifle Division

24th Rifle Division

228th Rifle Division

195th Rifle Division

3RD GUARDS ARMY

34th Guards Rifle Corps

59th Guards Rifle Division

61st Guards Rifle Division

279th Rifle Division

32nd Rifle Corps

259th Rifle Division

266th Rifle Division

8TH GUARDS ARMY

28th Guards Rifle Corps

39th Guards Rifle Division

79th Guards Rifle Division

88th Guards Rifle Division

29th Guards Rifle Corps

27th Guards Rifle Division

74th Guards Rifle Division

82nd Guards Rifle Division

33rd Rifle Corps

50th Rifle Division

78th Rifle Division

6TH ARMY

4th Guards Rifle Corps

47th Guards Rifle Division

57th Guards Rifle Division

26th Guards Rifle Corps

25th Guards Rifle Division

35th Guards Rifle Division

12TH ARMY

66th Rifle Corps

203rd Rifle Division

333rd Rifle Division

60th Guards Rifle Division

244th Rifle Division

1st Guards Mechanized Corps

1st Guards Mechanized Brigade

2nd Guards Mechanized Brigade

3rd Guards Mechanized Brigade

9th Guards Tank Brigade

23rd Tank Corps

3rd Tank Brigade

39th Tank Brigade

135th Tank Brigade

56th Motorized Rifle Brigade

17TH AIR ARMY

1st Guards Mixed Aviation Corps

1st Mixed Aviation Corps

9th Mixed Aviation Corps

SOUTHERN FRONT (Redesignated 4th Ukrainian Front from October 20, 1943)

Commander: Fyodor Tolbukhin

(See Red Army Order of Battle: 4th Ukrainian Front on page 71)

German Order of Battle

ARMY GROUP SOUTH

Commander: Erich von Manstein

Fourth Panzer Army

First Panzer Army

Eighth Army

Sixth Army

Luftflotte 2

Luftflotte 4

ARMY GROUP A

Commander: Ewald von Kleist

Seventeenth Army

Sixth Army

Romanian Cavalry Division

ARMY GROUP CENTER

Commander: Günther von Kluge

Second Army

(Army Group Center's part in the Dnieper battle was brief and operations halted on October 3, 1943)

As fighting intensified the Soviets increased their systematic shelling and bombing of the west bank of the river. The first bridgehead on the western shore was finally established on 22 September at the confluence of the Dnieper and Pripyat rivers, in the northern part of the front. In spite of heavy German fire, Soviet assault units utilized every available floating device to cross the river. On 24 and 25 September another bridgehead was created near Dniprodzerzhynsk, followed three days later at Kremenchuk.

Red Army troops storm the west bank of the Dnieper.

Soviet soldiers crossing the Dnieper with an artillery tractor. A Soviet artillery piece can be seen on the bank awaiting transportation.

On 28 September assaults were successfully made near Kremenchuk. By the end of September, 23 bridgeheads had been successfully established on the western side, with determined Soviet forces driving back German units some seven miles across the steppes and leaving them exposed to merciless attacks by Soviet fighter-bombers which annihilated them.

Under the watchful eye of their commanding officer Soviet riflemen and a Pulemyot Maxima PM 1910 machine-gunner fire at German troops attempting to cross the river.

A Red Army assault unit makes its way to the edge of the Dnieper River and provides covering fire for an amphibious attack. The west bank is engulfed in smoke following a systematic bombardment of German positions.

During the first ten days of October, the Red Army launched an attack against German positions at the great bend of the river, between Kremenchuk and Zaporozhye. The attack began with a massive artillery bombardment that pounded the German bridgehead. In no less than an hour the Germans counted some 15,000 shell bursts in their sector. German batteries replied in kind as far as they were able, but the main attack would fall on the infantry.

By 15 October, the Soviet 2nd Ukrainian Front had bulldozed its way through and crossed the river. Over the next few days, they poured divisions across the river and tore open the German front between the Eighth Army and the left wing of the First Panzer Army. On 18 October Soviet troops took Pyatikhatka, 35 miles south of the Dnieper, and cut the main rail lines to Dnepropetrovsk and Krivoi Rog. Soviet forces were now driving straight for Krivoi Rog, the supply and communication hub for Army Group South; additionally, the locomotives there were a vital asset for supply to the army group.

Manstein was determined that he could not allow the loss of Krivoi Rog and scraped together what he could muster to the stem the Soviet onslaught. He managed to find six weakened armored divisions, including the elite Waffen-SS Totenkopf Division which was put into line on the right flank of the Soviet advance. Even the SS units were hard pressed and did not receive the supplies of fresh men and armor they had been promised.

What followed was a massive counterthrust with Heer and Waffen-SS troops using all available reserves and resources to bitterly contest the Soviet advance. In the bloody battle that ensued the Germans, at great cost in men and materiel, managed to break up two Soviet armored corps and nine rifle divisions. The Red Army lost more than 300 tanks and 5,000 prisoners. The remaining Soviet forces in the area staggered back toward the Dnieper, allowing the exhausted German combat formations to temporarily stabilize the front. The troops were made fully aware of the significance of holding the vital city of Krivoi Rog, that the outcome would be the deciding factor in the future operations of Army Group South in the Crimea.

Farther north along the Dnieper Heer troops supported by Waffen-SS soldiers from the Das Reich Division had meanwhile been trying to prevent large numbers of enemy troops from consolidating control of areas west of the river and to stop the Soviets establishing a bridgehead. The SS Der Führer regiment seized the town of Grebeni, but at great cost: only 500 soldiers were left in its ranks. Still undeterred from the losses, Das Reich continued to fight a number of inconclusive battles in the region, which saw its subunits becoming even further depleted.

An 8cm Raketen-Vielfachwerfer launcher mounted on a self-propelled rocket projector vehicle during fighting along the Dnieper in the late summer of 1943. This was the German attempt to copy the Soviet Katyusha rocket launcher. The Germans took the 82mm rocket and supported it through a 24-rail assembly. These weapons were then bolted to halftrack vehicles for a self-propelled and mobile battlefield function.

In Profile:
T-34/85 Model 1943 & KV-85 Heavy Tank

T-34/85 Model 1943, September 1943

A T-34/85 tank in a field during operations in southern Ukraine. These Russian tanks were very successful against the Panzer divisions, and scored considerable hits against late variant Panzer IVs, Panthers, Tigers and numerous tank-hunters. (Oliver Missing)

KV-85 Heavy Tank, Zaporozhye, September 1943

This tank was an interim heavy tank solution to help combat the arrival of the German Panther medium tank series in 1943. However, its overall combat effectiveness was insubstantial, especially against heavier German tanks. Yet despite this, the tank was mass-produced and was successful in larger numbers. (Oliver Missing)

Out in the field during a lull in the fighting is an 8cm Granatwerfer 34 (8cm GrW 34) mortar crew. This weapon was the standard German infantry mortar during the war and was used extensively for both offensive and defensive operations.

Throughout the weeks that ominously followed, the German front lines were pulled farther westward with Heer and their Waffen-SS counterparts defending, attacking, and counterattacking as the situation demanded. A number of successful battles fought in this sector of the front were due to the efforts of determined troops, but came with a high price in blood. The unrelenting firepower and numerical superiority of the Red Army were staggering.

Consequently, during the final weeks of 1943, it appeared the Germans were incapable of sustaining their defensive positions along the Dnieper for any length of time. When Soviet assault troops attacked and established bridgeheads on the west bank, German troops dug

Heer troops in their winter whites pass a burning building during the withdrawal from the Dnieper.

During winter operations and a well-supplied 8.8cm FlaK 18 crew can be seen preparing their lethal weapon against a ground target. Note the pile of ammunition and the Sd.Ah.201 limber.

themselves into the clay of the banks. In spite of the situation, the Germans were determined to hold the west bank and launched significant counterattacks in order to cut off supply lines to the enemy bridgeheads.

Soviet losses on the bridgeheads were enormous with the majority of divisions losing almost half their men and equipment. However, despite the losses, Red Army units held and over the coming weeks massed Soviet forces poured across the river to support the bridgeheads. Fighting raged, but the Germans were overwhelmed.

In the latter part of October, the Soviets began drawing German forces away from the Lower Dnieper and from the city of Kiev. As the winter set in the front stagnated again, but by December the Red Army controlled a bridgehead almost 200 miles wide and 60 miles deep in a number of areas. In the south the Crimea was now cut off from the rest of the German forces and any hope of preventing the Soviets from advancing from the east bank of the Dnieper had been lost forever.

A FlaK crew clad in winter-reversibles during a fire mission against a ground target during defensive operations.

Dnieper–Carpathian Offensive, January–May 1944

The battle of the Dnieper had been a considerable strategic success for the Red Army in late 1943 with assault troops and armored columns from the 4th Ukrainian Front reaching the frozen banks on the lower reaches of the river around Kakhovka–Tsvurupinsk. Their fierce, fast, and unrelenting drive to the Dnieper had not only created a number of bridgeheads into the Western Ukraine, but also consequently cut off the German Seventeenth Army stationed in the Crimea.

With the east bank of the Dnieper in Soviet hands, plans were drawn up to unleash what the Red Army called "the liberation of right-bank Ukraine." This massive offensive was aimed at the southern section of the Soviet–German front which covered a vast area, from the Dnieper to the Carpathians, from Polsia to the Black Sea, encompassing the right-bank Ukraine, Western Ukraine, Crimea, and even parts of Moldova and Romania.

The terrain that sprawled out across the western bank of the Dnieper was diverse, ranging from miles of wooded swampy areas, to endless steppes, ravines, hills, and mountains. There were also many rivers, such as the Bug, Dniester, Prut, Ingulets, and Siret, all mainly flowing from the northwest to the southeast of the Ukraine.

A young Soviet soldier poses during operations in early 1944.

Inside in what appears to be a stationary Sd.Kfz.10 halftrack. A commanding officer can be seen sitting inside the armored vehicle whilst another officer scours the road through a pair of binoculars whilst a column of withdrawing halftracks passes by.

There was very little information on the region. Maps frequently showed none of the roads, and those that were shown were often in terrible state of repair. In 1941 when the Germans advanced into the region, they were totally ignorant of the area and unprepared. When the first rains came, they found that the bad roads immediately turned to mud. Horses, wheeled vehicles, and soldiers with their equipment ground to a halt in the quagmire. For hours, and sometimes days, units struggled to try and rescue their men and equipment. Tracked vehicles were often withdrawn from the line and brought back to tow stricken soldiers, sometimes up to their waist in mud trying to relieve vehicles and horses. Life for the Wehrmacht troops fighting in these conditions was an existence at a basic level. And three years later nothing had changed, except they were fighting an enemy who knew the region and was tactically diverse.

Although the conditions on the west bank of the Dnieper were hardly compatible with fast-moving combat operations, the terrain did allow Red Army formations to successfully launch broad offensive operations utilizing all their different types of assault troops, and armored and mechanized units. However, the territory the Soviets wanted to seize in the

A Waffen-SS Pz.Kpfw.III tankman sitting on the cupola converses with an officer during operations in January 1944. (NARA)

south was not just to drive out the German invaders; it was more than that. Stalin needed the Ukraine as it was economically and industrially important to Russia. The region produced iron and manganese ore, oil, sugar, maize, wheat, and beef. The Crimea also boasted the four important ports of Feodosiya, Kerch, Sevastopol, and Yevpatoria, which meant that the Soviets could secure their Black Sea Fleet in the central and western parts of the Black Sea.

Manstein was fully aware of the strategic importance of the right bank of the Ukraine and Crimea, as this vast region was the route into Poland and the Balkans. In order to defend

Soviet troops crossing the Dnieper River bound for Western Ukraine. The sign reads "Odessa 128km." In late March 1944, the 3rd Ukrainian Front was deployed to secure Odessa.

the area Army Group South and Army Group A put together two panzer and two field armies, from north to south. The Germans were supported by Hungarian and Romanian forces. In total were some 93 divisions including 18 panzer and four panzergrenadier divisions, two motorized brigades, three heavy panzer battalions of Tiger tanks, 18 Sturmgeschütz assault gun brigades, a battalion of Elefant tank destroyers, and a mixture of artillery and PaK battalions, including pioneer engineering units. Almost half of the German troops, and three-quarters of the Panzerwaffe that were employed on the Eastern Front were to take part in the defense of west-bank Ukraine. Manstein and Kleist wanted to withdraw these forces from the river line into better, impregnable defensive positions, but in spite of incessant requests to the Wolfschanze, the East Prussian HQ, Hitler blatantly refused. They would have to fight where they stood. However, Manstein and von Kleist tended to ignore the "Führer Order" and sent fictitious reports to commanders in the field, ordering them to conduct a series of withdrawals.

In front of the Germans stood the Soviet 1st, 2nd, 3rd, and 4th Ukrainian Fronts, supported by the 2nd Belorussian Front. The offensive was to be the first and only time during the entire war on the Eastern Front that six Soviet armies and elite mechanized armored formations would be used together in a single battle. It was one of the largest offensives of the war involving some 3,500,000 troops stretching along a front of 800 miles in length.

German soldiers wearing their reversible winter coats white side out sit around a campfire in a wooded area in Southern Ukraine, winter 1944.

47

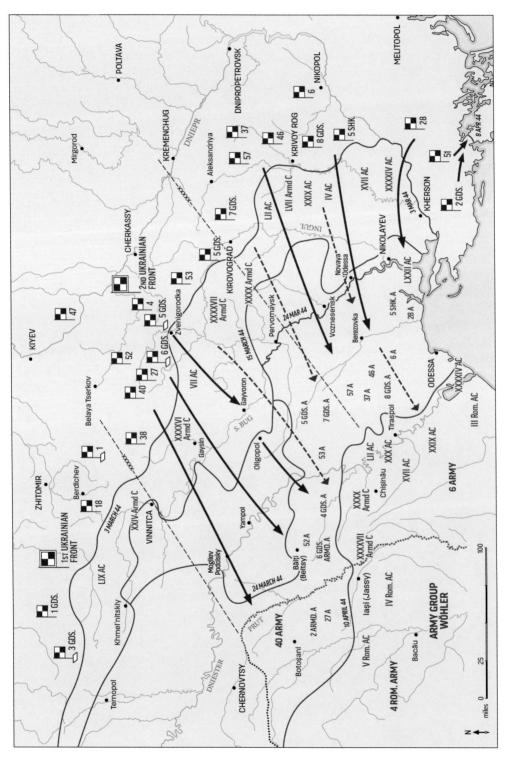

The Red Army advance through Central and Southern Ukraine during March and April 1944.

In Profile:
SS Grenadier, 5th SS Panzer Division Wiking & Motorcyclist With Sidecar Combination

SS Grenadier, 5th SS Panzer Division Wiking, Cherkassy, January 1944

This Waffen-SS grenadier wears the late-style, two-piece, insulated, reversible suit, plus the SS M43 cap. He is armed with the 7.9mm StG 44 assault rifle and a Panzerfaust. (Johnny Shumate)

Motorcyclist With Sidecar Combination

The motorcyclist belongs to the 2nd SS Panzer Division Das Reich. Note the *Wolfsangel* (Crampon, or lit. wolf-anchor) *Doppelhaken* (double hook) painted in white on the sidecar. There are many variations of this symbol, including both horizontal and vertical ones. The upright variation is called the *Donnerkeil* (lightning), and the horizontal variation is known as the werewolf. The *Wolfsangel* ancient runic symbol was widely used in Germany by several Nazi organizations and military units, including the Das Reich. (Johnny Shumate)

German infantry and a Panther tank loaded up with fuel drums stopped in a Ukrainian village.

In a former German tank ditch a Soviet 120mm M1943 "SAMOVAR" mortar crew in action.

German Order of Battle
ARMY GROUP SOUTH
Commander: Erich von Manstein

Fourth Panzer Army

First Panzer Army

Eighth Army

Sixth Army

Third Romanian Army

Fourth Romanian Army

First Hungarian Army

Red Army Order of Battle

1ST UKRAINIAN FRONT
Commander: Nikolai Vatutin

1st Guards Tank Army

6th Guards Tank Army

40th Guards Tank Army

60th Guards Tank

3rd Guards Army

1st Tank Army

4th Tank Army

18th Army

38th Army

2nd Air Army

2ND UKRAINIAN FRONT
Commander: Ivan Konev

4th Guards Army

7th Guards Army

27th Guards Army

53rd Guards Army

2nd Guard Tank Army

5th Guards Tank Army

5th Air Army

3RD UKRAINIAN FRONT
Commander: Rodion Malinovsky

8th Guards Army

37th Guards Army

46th Guards Army

57th Guards Army

6th Army (Reserve)

17th Air Army

4TH UKRAINIAN FRONT
Commander: Fyodor Tolbukhin

2nd Guards Army

5th Guards Army

Coastal Army and Black Sea Fleet

8th Air Army

A Pz.Kpfw.IV has evidently been knocked out of action by an enemy anti-tank shell. The tank's side skirts have almost been completely blown off from the impact and a dead crew member lies beside the vehicle partially covered in snow.

On Christmas Eve 1943, following a fortnight of the Germans preparing their defensive positions and the Soviets planning their attack across the Dnieper, the offensive was launched by the 1st Ukrainian Front against the German Fourth Army to the west and southwest of Kiev. All along the front Soviet units crashed into action, comprising sappers and infantry supported by heavy machine guns, mortars, and a number of tanks and self-propelled guns. Behind the assault detachments came advanced battalions, which were heavily supported by tank and self-propelled gun battalions.

Waffen-SS troops halted in a field next to an Sd.Kfz.251 halftrack. In spite of fierce resistance by the Wehrmacht in late February and early March, Army Group South was forced to make a slow fighting withdrawal to the Dniester River, on the Romanian border.

A Waffen-SS Sd.Kfz.251 passes a group of winter-glad SS grenadiers in Southern Ukraine. Some 11 German divisions, including the SS Wiking Division and the new Belgian Walloon volunteer unit, SS Sturmbrigade Wallonien, were used in an effort to try and stem the Soviet push through the Ukraine.

The Red Army soon had its powerful infantry and armored divisions positioned around Kiev and quickly recaptured Zhytomyr. West of Zhytomyr shell after shell thundered into the German strongpoints. In some sectors of the front German soldiers, fearing complete destruction, scrambled out of their trenches to save themselves from the rain of bombs.

One of the quickest and most effective means of moving armored units and complete divisions from one part of the front to another was by rail. Here Panthers have been hurriedly transferred by rail to Southern Ukraine in order to assist in its frenetic defense.

Halted on a icy road outside a Ukrainian village are two StuG.IIIs and an Sd.Kfz.251 armored personnel halftrack.

Along the whole front the Soviet artillery devoted the majority of its time to supporting the reconnaissance attacks and pulverizing the German defensive positions in depth. Although Manstein's forces defended well and slowed the enemy onslaught in a number of places, most German units were pushed back some 100 miles. Their fighting withdrawal proved to be successful, but it was a temporary measure. Tactically, it was a slow painful retreat that

A column of Panther tanks bound for the front. Large parts of Western Ukraine thawed earlier than usual, turning the roads and surrounding fields into a quagmire.

German winter-clad grenadiers including an MG42 machine gunner march through the snow, passing an abandoned Russian BM-13N Katyusha on a Lend-Lease US6 truck. A German 3-ton Sd.Kfz.11 can be seen halted behind it.

was rapidly spiraling out of control, draining all available German reserves and resources. The techniques that were now employed in the south by Manstein were stemming the fresh enemy offensive and delaying the ultimate collapse of Army Group South.

Over the course of the first week of January 1944, the operation saw the Red Army making considerable gains against German defensive positions. In that week a number of Soviet units advanced to a depth of nearly 60 miles, completely clearing German forces from the Kiev and Zhytomyr regions, including several districts in and around Vinnitsa and Rovno. In fact, the Red Army offensive was so swift that Army Group South's northern flank was threatened with being cut off which would prevent units escaping from the Ukraine into Poland. In order to avert a catastrophe and plug the gaps in the German lines and halt the enemy offensive on the northern flank, the Germans had to urgently transfer 12 divisions of the First Panzer Army from Southern Ukraine to the area. The reserves that finally arrived were badly depleted which further affected the conduct of operations.

On January 5, the 2nd Ukrainian Front moved into position and began its attack by launching what was known as the Kirovograd Offensive. One of its first objectives was to stem the III Panzer Corps attacks which were causing considerable problems for the Soviet advance in the Kirovograd region. Losses to both German troops and armor were massive. In order to avert a complete catastrophe in the area, Manstein flew to the Wolfschanze, frantically requesting Hitler's permission to withdraw, but this was again refused.

What followed on the battlefield saw strong Soviet forces attempting to smash German positions around the town of Kirovograd. By January 8 the town fell, but the Soviets soon found German resistance in the area stronger than expected. Some 11 German divisions, including the SS Panzer Division Wiking and the new Belgian Walloon volunteer unit, SS Sturmbrigade Wallonien, which had recently been transferred from the Heer to SS control, were embroiled in a drastic attempt to stem the Soviet push west. Here these German divisions held a salient into the Soviet lines between the towns of Korsun and Cherkassy. Despite repeated warnings from Manstein, Hitler continually refused to allow the exposed units to be pulled back to safety.

On January 18, Manstein was proved right when Vatutin's 1st Ukrainian Front and Konev's 2nd Ukrainian Front attacked the forward lines of the salient and surrounded two German corps. Trapped in what was known as the "Korsun pocket" were some 50,000 men, a total of six German divisions, including the elite SS Wiking and the SS Sturmbrigade Wallonien. The trapped forces were designated Gruppe Stemmerman after its commander. The Wiking division was the only armored unit in the pocket with some 43 tanks and assault guns. Two assault gun battalions provided an additional 27 assault guns. With these tanks and assault guns they were ordered to drive the Soviets back and produce an impossible effort by breaking out of the encirclement and destroying the enemy. Day and night the fighting raged, but the Soviets with some 35 divisions around the salient inflicted terrible casualties. The constant pressure gradually saw the pocket shrink to some 40 square miles by early February.

As disaster loomed a relief effort was quickly assembled. The 1st SS Panzer Division Leibstandarte was rushed to the area. Oberstleutnant Franz Bake's Tiger tanks of the 503rd Heavy Tank Battalion were ordered to help wrench open the pocket. However, the Tiger tanks and supporting vehicles found the terrain problematic: an unseasonable rise in temperature had caused a sudden thaw and turned the terrain into a boggy morass, making movement almost impossible in some areas. Nevertheless, deep in mud, the SS pushed forward supported by Heer units, and by February 8 elements of the Leibstandarte and the 16th Panzer Division had reached and established bridgeheads across the Gniloi Tickich River, west of Boyarka. Gruppe Stemmerman began immediately pulling back troops from the north of the *kessel* (pocket, lit. cauldron), and attacked south to link up with the relief forces on the north bank of the Gniloi Tickich.

By February 13 the spearheads of the panzer divisions were within reach of the encircled troops, but were exhausted by their efforts, and ground to a halt on the Lysanka–Oktyar–Chisinzy line. Hitler at last relented and consented to the evacuation of the Korsun pocket.

The crew of a whitewashed StuG 40 Ausf G complete with intact side skirts pose for the camera during winter operations in 1944.

A 15cm s.IG33 heavy infantry gun being prepared for a fire mission. This gun was regarded as a Wehrmacht workhorse and could be operated by specially trained infantrymen.

On the night of February 16, Gruppe Stemmerman received a communiqué from Manstein ordering it to break out of the pocket at all costs. As Heer and SS troops began to move slowly across the boggy terrain, the Soviets quickly became aware of what was happening and opened up with a thunderous barrage. Hundreds of Soviet guns of all calibers poured a storm of fire onto the German positions.

Destruction inside the pocket was so severe that the wounded had to be left behind, as did most of the artillery and heavy equipment. SS Sturmbrigade Wallonien suffered terrible losses covering the rearguard, with almost three-quarters of its entire strength left dead on the battlefield. As the remnants inched nearer the German lines, Soviet fire intensified, inflicting further casualties. In typical Waffen-SS style, the Wiking Division's only remaining tanks turned back and fought to the death whilst the last of the brigade reached the German lines. The SS Das Reich too was another combat formation that had been rushed to help relieve the troops in the pocket. They were among the rearguard units holding fast while the bulk of the encircled troops made good their escape. Das Reich suffered heavy losses as a result of their self-sacrifice. Out of 5,000 troops deployed to the area, some 1,121 of all

During a snow blizzard and German grenadiers can be seen standing next to a knocked-out Soviet ISU-152. Note one of the soldiers armed with the Panzerfaust.

A Pz.Kpfw.IV panzer crew have halted along a road with the rest of their column and can be seen with a map conferring on their next operational move.

ranks were killed in action. In spite of the huge losses in men and equipment, some 33,000 German troops had escaped with their lives. Another major disaster had been averted in Southern Russia.

During March, Army Group South was forced to make a slow fighting withdrawal to the Dniester River, on the border with Romania. On March 11, parts of the SS Totenkopf Division that had been fighting fanatically supporting Heer units was pulled back to the Dniester. It was then airlifted to Balta to form the core of a new defensive front there.

As the Soviets resumed their offensive toward the Dniester, both Waffen-SS and Heer divisions, shattered from weeks of intensive combat, continued doggedly to defend every foot of ground. All along the battered front there was no respite. The Soviet offensive tore a

A column of side-car combinations can be seen bucketing along a dusty road, probably during a reconnaissance exercise. Note the motorcyclists are wearing aviator goggles to protect their eyes from the dust.

massive hole between the First and Fourth Panzer Armies at Proskurov. Before the gap could be successfully sealed, the entire First Panzer Army, together with units from Das Reich and Leibstandarte, found itself totally encircled in a huge pocket near Kamenets–Podolsky. In the long, fierce battle that ensued the Germans recaptured Isyaslavl and stemmed the Red Army drive. Fighting around the town raged until March 14, by which time losses to the battered grenadier companies had become so severe that they could no longer hold their lines. As the situation deteriorated further across the area, panic-stricken front-line commanders pleaded for the release of the last reserves to restore the situation. At this point

A mortar crew sighting their 120mm mortar. This mortar could be broken down into three parts—the barrel, bipod, and base plate—and transported short distances by infantry. For longer distances it was towed by a GAZ-66 truck on a two-wheeled tubular carriage.

A group of motorcyclists have halted on a road during a reconnaissance exercise. Throughout the war on the Eastern Front, motorcyclists played an important role either as couriers, scouting duties, tank hunters, or in divisions of rifle troops.

Hitler agreed and allowed at once for the II SS Panzer Corps, which consisted of the 9th SS Panzer Division Hohenstaufen and the 10th SS Panzer Division Frundsberg, to be rushed to the Eastern Front from France.

Whilst Hohenstaufen and Frundsberg boarded the long trains bound for Southern Russia, Manstein's forces were being slowly bled to death inside the Kamenets–Podolsky pocket. Tons of ammunition and fuel were being hurriedly airlifted into the *kessel* in order to prevent Manstein from abandoning all his heavy equipment and armor when the time came to break out. When the two new SS divisions arrived, they quickly launched a flank attack that smashed onto the tip of the Soviet spearhead and allowed the trapped First Panzer Army to escape the slaughter. As it fought its way out toward the west, the two SS divisions linked up and counterattacked in a relentless battle to take the pressure off the retreating panzer army.

By early April, the First Panzer Army was limping southwest from the smoldering pocket and linked up with the Fourth Panzer Army. Both were in terrible shape from weeks of heavy fighting. To make matters worse, Hitler blamed the depletion of these once-powerful formations on what he called the "lack of strategic tactics" of Manstein and Kleist. The Soviet success in the area, he said, was the result of his commanders' poor planning. As a result, he sacked both Manstein and Kleist and replaced them with Walter Model and Ferdinand Schörner, and renamed the army groups North Ukraine and South Ukraine.

Hitler then made it very clear to his new commanders that the sole objective on the southern front was to recapture the Ukraine at all costs. He told Model and Schörner that he had adopted what was called the "Shield and Sword" policy which espoused that retreats were only tolerable if they paved the way for a counterstroke. Hitler assumed that his policy would cost the enemy more casualties than were necessary, a crucial contemplation in the face of vital German manpower shortages. Model felt the strategy seemed to make some sense and appeared promising in theory, but he was aware that his forces had lost their advantage in mobility and particularly in the air. Another problem was that the defense, which the Germans had deemed formidable, was not that threatening to the enemy. Quite often Red Army units decided to simply bypass German defenses and reduce the pockets at a later date. The Soviet aerial and firepower superiority simply left German forces vulnerable to relentless bombardments and huge losses.

Hitler's new doctrine could offer little more than to delay the inevitable. Although the battles that raged on the right bank of the Dnieper were the most important events in 1944, by April the Germans were struggling to retain cohesion. The situation was made worse when the Red Army captured the Lvov–Odessa rail line, which was the main life support of Army Group South. As a consequence, the Soviets were able to prize open positions around Lvov an advance toward eastern Poland, which was the basis for the Lvov–Sandomierz Offensive.

Signs of disintegration now plagued every sector of the German front. By early May the situation in many areas of Army Group South was almost impossible to control. Although a number of sectors held their ground, large parts of the front were on the point of collapse. No less than one Luftwaffe and nine infantry divisions had slowly and systematically bled to death on the battlefield. Seven panzer and panzergrenadier, one Fallschirmjager, and two infantry divisions were so badly mauled that they were withdrawn from the front and sent to the west for R&R. The remnants of the divisions were in appalling shape with many losing

A 2cm Flak 38 defensive position. This was one of a number of defenses erected by the Germans west of the Dnieper River. Note the partially dug wooden building complete with windows. The gun is well emplaced and probably overlooking miles of terrain down to the river.

Shirtless 12 cm Granatwerfer 42 troops are seen preparing their large mortar for action.

significant amounts of equipment and soldiers. In fact, the condition of the majority of the divisions was so bad that 18 of the 39 divisions belonging to Army Group A were unable to reinforce its regiments with reserves and were hastily diluted into *Kampfgruppen*.

In spite of the state of Army Group A, another territory that was crucial to retain was the Crimea. As with right-bank Ukraine, the Crimea was of the greatest political, economic, and strategic importance to both the German and the Soviet war machines. With the bulk of the Germans fighting west of the Dnieper, the Red Army took advantage of the situation and launched a series of offensive actions in order to recapture German-held Crimea. What followed was known as the battle of the Crimea.

In Profile:
T-34/85 Model 1943 & Sd.Kfz. 3b Maultier Halftrack

T-34/85 Model 1943, February 1944

A whitewashed T-34/85 on the west bank of the Dnieper. Initially the T-34/85 was found in the elite Red Guards battalions, which, up to December 1943, were in training and did not see battle proper until early 1944. By the spring of that year around 400 had been delivered to front-line units and instantly became popular with the crews. (Oliver Missing)

Sd.Kfz. 3b Maultier Halftrack, May 1944

This vehicle, complete with mounted 2cm Flak 38 antiaircraft gun, was converted from a Ford V3000S as a result of the disastrous experiences of the Wehrmacht on the Eastern Front. Because standard German trucks could not cope with the Soviet terrain and roads, especially during the spring thaw, it led to the Germans adapting standard trucks. This vehicle carries a summer camouflage scheme of a three-tone system of green and brown over a sand base color. (Oliver Missing)

Battle of the Crimea, April–May 1944

In late 1943 the winter did nothing to impede the Soviet offensives in the south from grinding farther west. During this period the Wehrmacht was under considerable pressure to retain its position between the Black Sea and the Sea of Azov. For 10 months the Germans had secured a

A battery of 10.5cm le.FH18 guns positioned in a wood. A gun crew is preparing for action. Below, the gun is being fired.

One of the most standardised divisional anti-tank guns in the German inventory was the 7.5cm PaK40. Here the weapon is being loaded for action, well concealed in undergrowth.

bridgehead on the Taman Peninsula, known as the Kuban bridgehead, which was a heavily fortified position and originally intended to be used by German forces to undertake renewed attacks towards the oilfields of the Caucasus.

Red Army troops in the Crimea. Here a Maxim M1910 machine-gun crew is in action.

Defending the bridgehead was the Seventeenth Army comprising the Wetzel Group which consisted of the X Army Corps under the command of General Wilhelm Wetzel, XXXXIV Army Corps, XXXXIX Army Corps, and a Romanian corps, comprising six German and two Romanian divisions which were deployed along the 100-mile front from Novorossiysk to Kurchanskaya. Despite the many combat units at its disposal, the Seventeenth Army was under considerable strain due to reduced manpower and a shortage of materiel. The combined German and Romanian forces totaled some 200,000 men in mid-1943, but were defending positions against a much superior enemy force consisting of 69 units with a combined strength of more than 350,000 men.

During the second half of 1943 the Seventeenth Army found itself under heavy and persistent attack from the Red Army. Fighting was bitter and bloody; under unrelenting Soviet air and ground bombardments, in October 1943, remnants of the Seventeenth Army began to withdraw from the Kuban bridgehead across the strait to Crimea.

During the weeks and months that followed, massive Soviet firepower continued rolling back the German forces in Southern Ukraine. By November the Red Army had eventually cut off the land-based conduit of the Seventeenth Army through the Perekop Isthmus. Hitler immediately thwarted any plans of the Seventeenth Army evacuating its troops by sea. He made it very clear that the beleaguered Wehrmacht stand firm and fortify the Crimean Peninsula.

The crew of a StuG 40 pose for the camera whilst the vehicle is being re-tracked.

Bound for Sevastopol, Don Cossacks hitch a ride on a T-34 tank from the 19th Tank Corps, April 1944.

By the end of 1943, the Soviets were landing troops across the Kerch Strait, attempting to retake the peninsula, but apart from gaining a toehold in the Kerch region, they achieved little. German defenses in the Crimea stood firm, with a defense in depth of some 195,000 troops. Furthermore, supplies were bolstered by German and Romanian ships that shuttled

A Granatwerfer sGW 42 mortar crew prepares for action. This deadly 12cm heavy mortar was developed in response to the Soviet mortar of the same caliber and was a virtual copy of the Red Army weapon.

An interesting photograph showing two stationary Sd.Kfz 4 Panzerwerfer 42 on a muddy road. It appears both vehicles have developed mechanical problems, probably due to overheating. These vehicles were largely distributed to the Nebeltruppen which formed Nebelwerfer batteries. They were considerably effective in the Ukraine and attached organically to infantry units.

between Romania and Sevastopol. The Soviet Navy feared venturing out from the western coast of the Crimea, concerned it would be attacked by Stukas or coastal artillery batteries. Instead, over the coming weeks, Red Army ground units concentrated attacking the neck of the Crimea and amassing its forces for a full-scale offensive against the peninsula. By the end of March 1944, the Soviets had assembled a force of some 470,000 troops for a decisive assault.

In a muddy field, a Maultier Sd.Kz.3 is re-supplying vital ammunition to a Hummel Sd.kz.165. The Hummel often served in armored artillery battalions or *Panzerartillerie Abteilungen* of the panzer divisions. They were divided into heavy self-propelled artillery batteries, each with six Hummel and one ammunition carrier.

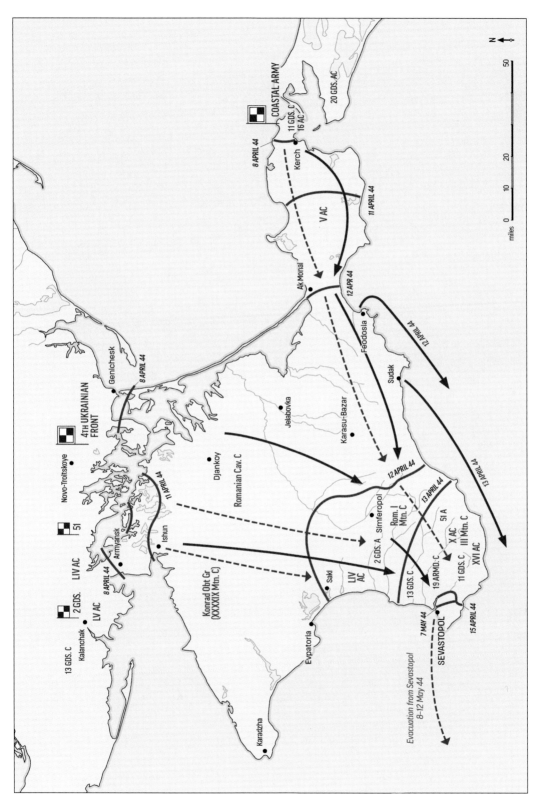

The final battle in the Crimea during April and May 1944

In Profile:
Ilyushin Il-2 Shturmovik & Destroyed Ilyushin Il-2 Shturmovik

Ilyushin Il-2 Shturmovik, Sevastopol, Crimea, May 1944

The Il-2 was never given an official name and *shturmovik* is the Russian word meaning ground-attack aircraft. These aircraft were used extensively in Southern Russia, continuously bombing and machine-gunning German columns and defensive positions. (Oliver Missing)

Destroyed Ilyushin Il-2 Shturmovik, Sevastopol, Crimea, May 1944

During the German defense of Sevastopol antiaircraft guns managed to knock out a number of Il-2 Shturmovik aircraft. (Oliver Missing)

German Order of Battle
ARMY GROUP A

Commander: Ferdinand Schörner

SEVENTEENTH ARMY

Romanian Mountain Corps

1st Mountain Division

2nd Mountain Division

Red Army Order of Battle
4TH UKRAINIAN FRONT

35th Tank-destroyer Artillery Brigade

530th Tank-destroyer Artillery Regiment

4th Guards Mortar Brigade

19th Tank Corps

6th Guards Tank Brigade

17th Guards Mine Battalion

102nd Pontoon-bridge Battalion

2nd Guard Army

13th Guards Rifle Corps

3rd Guards Rifle Division

24th Guards Rifle Division

87th Guards Rifle Division

54th Rifle Corps

126th Rifle Division

315th Rifle Division

387th Rifle Division

55th Rifle Corps

87th Rifle Division

347th Rifle Division

116th Fortified Region

2nd Guards Breakthrough Artillery Division

51st Army

1st Guards Rifle Corps

10th Rifle Corps

63rd Rifle Corps

77th Rifle Division

78th Fortified Region

26th Artillery Division

2nd Anti-aircraft Artillery Division

15th Anti-aircraft Artillery Division

18th Anti-aircraft Artillery Division

A dusty MG 42 machine-gunner. Although a machine-gun troop was normally a three-man squad, due to the high casualty rates suffered in Southern Russia it was commonly reduced to just two, but was still highly effective.

On April 7 the 4th Ukrainian Front began its assault across the neck of the peninsula. The Seventeenth Army soon began to buckle under the weight of enemy firepower. General Andrey Yeryomenko's Coastal Army reached Kerch a few days later as the Seventeenth Army retreated toward Sevastopol. Their withdrawal saw them burn everything in their wake as they fought through villages and towns, across a rocky landscape hosting precipitous slopes, narrow valleys, and hanging ravines. The Germans hoped that they would be evacuated by sea from the port of Sevastopol, but Hitler had ordered that the area be defended indefinitely: no fighting troops were to be evacuated.

General Schörner, commander of Army Group A, appealed to Hitler to rescind his decision. However, the Führer would only allow the evacuation of noncombatants.

Red Army troops advancing through Crimea pass abandoned German materiel on the route to Sevastopol.

Soviet troops in action in Sevastopol.

Instead, what was left of the Seventeenth Army, namely General Rudolf Konrad's XXXXIX Mountain Corps and General Karl Allmendinger's V Corps, with a total of five German and six Romanian divisions plus a Flak division, were expected to hold the line. However, the army had no armored formations and only two assault artillery brigades. The XXXXIX Mountain Corps held the northern part of the peninsula, including the "Tartarenwall" defenses across the Perekop Isthmus, with V Corps on the Kerch Peninsula containing the small Soviet bridgehead held by the Separate Coastal Army.

Red Army troops crossing Sivash Bay into the Crimea in late April.

Commander of the Seventeenth Army General Jaenecke led his beleaguered force in the Crimea against overwhelming Soviet superiority. He was sacked by Hitler for demanding either reinforcements or evacuation.

For some considerable time, the Seventeenth Army had been supplied by air and sea without any major Red Army interference, but it was now in danger of being totally isolated and supply lines cut off. During mid-April Soviet forces pounded the front lines and advanced across the Crimea causing considerable loss to heavy German materiel. Without artillery support or antitank guns, the German troops were routed in the face of the enemy armored attacks. In fact, in some divisions there were only 200 men capable of combat, a tenth of the 1941 strength. Battle-hardened infantrymen had become a rarity and most troops manning the forward positions were inexperienced. When units did receive orders to withdraw, it was often too late to move what vital equipment they had. Instead, soldiers frequently fled on foot pursued by Soviet armored and motorized forces. In some sectors, regimental artillery and heavy weapons companies had no option but to destroy their infantry guns, antitank guns, and mortars as they lacked the means to move them. Soon after this, units disappeared entirely from the order of battle. The Germans found it impossible to rely on their Romanian allies to help support the crumbling lines; many of their units simply disintegrated.

Of the three Soviet armies, the 2nd Guards Army successfully advanced at breakneck speed to the south through the Perekop Isthmus and through western Crimea, whilst the 51st Army drove through central Crimea to take Simferopol. Simultaneously, the Separate Coastal Army advanced southwest through eastern Crimea, linking up with the 51st Army at Karasubazar on 14 April. By 16 April Soviet forces had captured most of Crimea's strategic areas, including Yalta and Sudak on the southeast coast. Two days later the Separate Coastal Army was absorbed into the 4th Ukrainian Front as General Kondrat Melnik's

Captured and wounded German troops in the Crimea, early May.

Coastal Army. By 20 April Soviet artillery was already within striking range of Sevastopol, making the withdrawal of German troops to the city more hazardous. As the situation became increasingly desperate, Schörner felt that he had no option but to fly to Germany and ask Hitler once again for permission for the abandonment of Crimea. Alternatively, he

Wounded German troops who have escaped the Crimea arrive at the port of Constanza in Bulgaria.

requested immediate reinforcements or they must evacuate all fighting troops and naval personnel immediately. Hitler agreed to reinforce and told the general that his troops must hold Sevastopol for eight weeks until the Western Allies had executed their landings in North-West Europe and the strategic situation was therefore clarified. The Romanian forces, he said, would be evacuated followed by noncombat personnel.

Over the next few days reinforcements trickled through to the Crimea, but the Seventeenth Army was now trapped. Disorganized remnants were now compelled *to* set to work on the defense of Sevastopol. Morale, in spite the terrible situation, was unexpectedly good, for the majority of the German troops believed that when all the German naval, air force and administrative personnel had been evacuated after the Romanians, they would be next. However, German confidence soon diminished when on April 24 the remnants of the five German divisions were told that the Führer had ordered that Sevastopol be held to the last. On the same day, raging with anger, commander of the Seventeenth Army, General Erwin Jaenecke, flew to meet Hitler. The general was not one told hold his tongue and had already had two stormy meetings with the Führer over the situation. In an angry outburst Jaenecke bluntly demanded of Hitler two divisions of reinforcements and freedom of action. As a result of the meeting, the general was relieved of his command forthwith.

By late April the Red Army had pushed through to Sevastopol. Assaulting the city was by no means an easy task. Inside the city were five determined divisions that had made use of whatever they could muster to defend themselves, protected by defenses that comprised antitank obstacles, mines, and an assortment of barricades with a number of other bunker installations and strongpoints.

Assault troops belonging to the 2nd Taman Guards Division secure the Kerch Peninsula bridgehead; they are armed with the famous the PPSh-41 "Shpagin's machine-pistol."

The evacuation of noncombat personnel from Sevastopol began in earnest on April 12. Nine merchant ships and the entirety of the Kriegsmarine Black Sea Fleet were involved in the operation.

Red Army commanders were aware that the German defense of the port was essentially inadequate, but planned a systematic aerial and ground bombardment before the infantry attacked. The Soviet Air Force dropped 2,000 tons of bombs on the fortress and over the course of a number of days barrage after barrage pounded the city methodically. The merciless shelling had no pattern. It was aimless and incessant, but with each minute it seemed to increase in intensity. Mortars and the terrifying Katyushas soon added to cacophony. Once the artillery finally fell silent, the Soviet troops moved forward from their jump-off points and began the long-awaited infantry attack. Inside the fortress the Germans were assaulted from all sides. Fighting was brutal with both sides incurring terrible casualties. Fearing another repeat of Stalingrad, German commanders again begged Hitler for an evacuation. Permission was once again denied, in spite of the serious losses.

On May 5, the 2nd Guards Army began assaulting the well-dug-in German units, but due to the severity of the attacks the Germans could not hold their lines and were drawn off to the north, while the 51st Army and the Coastal Army attacked in the south at Sapun Hill.

Captured German troops being marched along the coast.

Soviet Marines overlooking Kerch, May 1944.

A T-34 9 operating in Lenin Street, Sevastopol, during operations on 9 May.

Two days later the hill was captured. Slowly and systematically German defensive positions were destroyed and the front lines reluctantly abandoned, leaving isolated groups of troops to fight to the death.

By May 8, the Soviets had penetrated the heart the city. German units left in the rubble-strewn streets were either destroyed or escaped westward, doggedly fighting from one fixed position to another. Under a hurricane of Soviet bombardments the Germans then fled

A T-34 tank on the liberation of Sevastopol. Note the Soviet naval flag on the turret.

Red Army troops occupying Sevastopol amidst abandoned German materiel.

toward the open Chersones Peninsula to make a last stand in the hope of being evacuated by sea.

As desperation gripped the German retreat onto the peninsula, on May 9, Hitler finally agreed to the evacuation of the remaining German forces. However, the task was almost impossible. Shipping sent out across the Black Sea to try and evacuate the stranded soldiers were attacked with many of the vessels sunk. Those troops waiting to be evacuated were bombed and strafed by Soviet fighter-bombers.

Red Army troops fire their guns into the air to celebrate the capture of Sevastopol. The bay is littered with damaged and destroyed German vessels

Soviet Marines usher ashore captured German naval ratings at Sevastopol.

On May 3, Axis strength in Sevastopol was 64,700 German and Romanian troops, of whom 10,000 were wounded and evacuated. The fate of the others is unknown. It is likely that they were either killed or captured. The rest of the Seventeenth Army in the Crimea managed to escape the slaughter. However, German losses during the Soviet offensive were significant: 77,500 were either dead or missing and 29,000 German and 7,000 Romanian troops were captured. Around 130,000 were evacuated by sea and 21,000 by air.

On May 25 the Soviet flag was hoisted over Sevastopol.

In Profile:
Borgward B 3000 & 152mm Howitzer M1937 (ML-20)

Borgward B 3000, Crimea, April 1944

This 3-ton medium-sized truck was a German supply vehicle capable of carrying a multitude of supplies as well as infantry and weaponry to the front. It is painted in a base color of dark yellow. (Oliver Missing)

152mm Howitzer M1937 (ML-20), Sapun Hill, Crimea, May 6, 1944

This Soviet howitzer was used extensively on the Eastern Front, primarily for indirect fire against enemy personnel, fortifications, and other key objectives in the near rear. Army regiments were allocated 18 ML-20s each; by 1945, artillery brigades in Guards armies had 36 ML-20s. (Oliver Missing)

Lvov–Sandomierz Offensive, July–August 1944

During the first week of June 1944, reports multiplied as news reached the various German commands that the Soviets were preparing a new summer offensive on the central front. By the morning of June 22, 1944, the third anniversary of the invasion of Russia, the long-awaited Red Army offensive was launched against Army Group Center. In total, the 1st Baltic and 3rd Belorussian Fronts utilized more than 2.5 million troops, 4,000 tanks, 25,000 artillery pieces and mortars, and 5,300 aircraft, to the northwest and southwest of Vitebsk. In opposition the Germans could only field 1,200,000 men, 9,500 guns, and 900 tanks, with around 1,300 aircraft.

The Soviet offensive was codenamed Operation *Bagration*, and within 24 hours of the launch Soviet forces had smashed through the lines of Army Group Center. Within a matter of days, the entire length of a 200-mile front stretching from Ostrov on the Lithuanian border to Kovel on the edge of the Pripet Marshes had been completely overrun. In just 12 days

T-34 tanks at a railhead in the Ukraine as Konev's 1st Ukrainian Front prepares to unleash its armored might to liberate Lvov and establish a number of bridgeheads on the Vistula River.

A crewmember loading ammunition into an Elefant in the Ukraine during the summer of 1944. Whilst this was a powerful German tank destroyer, the Red Army had produced a handbook on how to kill these tanks, showing weak spots and the distance required for Russian tank crews to successfully penetrate its thick armor.

A column of camouflaged Marder IIs make its way to the front.

Red Army assault troops supported by T-34 tanks attack a German position.

Army Group Center lost 25 divisions. As the Germans pulled back to save themselves from complete destruction, the Red Army continued its remorseless drive west, carving its way to the borders of East Prussia and Poland.

The reverberations caused by the *Bagration* offensive sent shockwaves into Army Group South. However, what made the situation worse for the Germans was that most of the Soviet forces and resources were allocated, not to *Bagration*'s Belorussian operations, but the Lvov–Sandomierz operations. Red Army commanders had been fully aware that by concentrating their forces in southern Poland and Ukraine, they were able to draw important German mobile reserves south, leaving Army Group Center vulnerable to collapse. As predicted, when Army Group Center buckled under the sheer weight of the Soviet onslaught, they watched powerful German panzer forces hastily being transferred back to the central front, leaving the Red Army free to pursue their objectives in seizing Western Ukraine, the Vistula bridgeheads, and gaining a foothold in Romania.

A young Russian soldier with his PPSh-41 "Shpagin's machine-pistol."

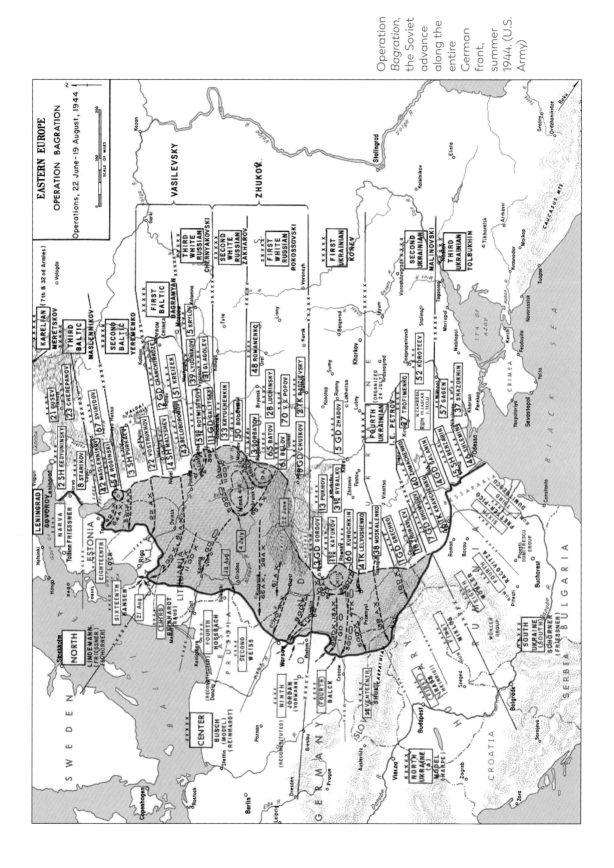

Operation *Bagration,* the Soviet advance along the entire German front, summer 1944. (U.S. Army)

Soviet halftracks towing ordnance along a typical road on the Eastern Front. Following a downpour, the roads were quickly turned into a quagmire, even in the summer months.

A Waffen-SS MG 42 machine-gun position. (NARA)

In Profile:
Tiger II, 501st Heavy Tank Battalion & Tiger I

Tiger II, 501st Heavy Tank Battalion, Defense of Sandomierz, July 29, 1944

The heavy armor and powerful long-range gun gave the Tiger II an advantage against all opposing Soviet tanks attempting to engage it head-on. It was very successful in both defensive and offensive operations. However, during early August 1944, two Tiger IIs were captured by the Soviets near Sandomierz, and were later moved to the testing grounds at Kubinka. This vehicle has a summer camouflage scheme of dark yellow sand base with thick patches of olive green and red brown over its entire armor and gun barrel. (Oliver Missing)

Tiger I, Defense of Lvov, July 22, 1944

A Tiger I with a full application of *zimmerit* antimine paste. During this period of the war, these vehicles constantly demonstrated both the lethalness of their 8.8cm guns and their invulnerability against Soviet antitank shells. However, there were too few to make any significant impact on their enemy. The vehicle has a summer camouflage scheme of dark yellow sand base with oversprayed patches of olive green and red brown. (Oliver Missing)

By mid-1943 divisional ant-tank and artillery units lacked considerable amounts of armored vehicles to tow their ordnance. Consequently much of it was pulled by animal draught as depicted in this photograph showing a PaK crew.

Thirsty Heer soldiers pause to drink water.

German Order of Battle
ARMY GROUP NORTH UKRAINE

Commander: Josef Harpe

18th Artillery Division

Luftflotte 4

VIII Fliegerkorps

Luftflotte 6

FOURTH PANZER ARMY

XLVI Panzer Corps

16th Panzer Division

17th Panzer Division

291st Infantry Division

340th Infantry Division

XXXXII Army Corps

72nd Infantry Division

88th Infantry Division

LVI Panzer Corps

26th Infantry Division

342nd Infantry Division

1st Ski Jäger Division

VIII Corps

5th Jäger Division

211th Infantry Division

12th Hungarian Reserve Division

FIRST PANZER ARMY

XIII Army Corps

361st Infantry Division

454th Security Division

14th Waffen Grenadier Division of the SS (1st Ukrainian)

XXXXVIII Panzer Corps

96th Infantry Division

349th Infantry Division

359th Infantry Division

III Panzer Corps

1st Panzer Division

8th Panzer Division

XXIV Panzer Corps

20th Panzergrenadier Division

100th Jäger Division

75th Infantry Division

254th Infantry Division

371st Infantry Division

LIX Army Corps

1st Infantry Division

208th Infantry Division

20th Hungarian Infantry Division

FIRST HUNGARIAN ARMY

<u>XI Army Corps</u>

101st Jäger Division

24th Hungarian Infantry Division

25th Hungarian Infantry Division

18th Hungarian Reserve Division

<u>VI Hungarian Army Corps</u>

27th Hungarian Light Division

1st Hungarian Mountain Brigade

Hungarian First Army Reserve

2nd Hungarian Panzer Division

2nd Hungarian Mountain Brigade

19th Hungarian Reserve Division

<u>VII Hungarian Army Corps</u>

16th Hungarian Infantry Division

68th Infantry Division

168th Infantry Division

Red Army Order of Battle

1st Ukrainian Front

Commander: Ivan Konev

3rd Guards Army

1st Guards Tank Army

13th Army

60th Army

38th Army

3rd Guards Tank Army

4th Tank Army

2nd Air Army

8cm Raketen-Vielfachwerfer launcher mounted on a self-propelled rocket projector vehicle. Batteries of these weapons were employed in defensive positions in the Ukraine and enjoyed a high kill rate.

By the time the Soviets had unleashed *Bagration*, Model's Army Group North Ukraine had already been forced to withdraw west of the Dnieper and was frantically trying to cling onto the northwestern regions of the Ukraine. As German units battled along a series of defensive lines, Stalin ordered his forces to liberate the Ukraine at all costs. Even before *Bagration* had been launched the Soviet high command had been planning what would become known as the Lvov–Sandomierz operation. Initially the offensive was titled the Lvov–Przemyśl Operation, the sole objective of which was for Konev's 1st Ukrainian Front to liberate Lvov and destroy all German troop concentrations left in the Ukraine and capture a number of bridgeheads on the Vistula River. Konev's operation was supposed to coincide with *Bagration*, but due to logistical problems and strong panzer formations moving between the central and southern fronts, it was delayed.

Instead, this gave Konev additional time to muster a million soldiers, 2,000 tanks, and 16,000 guns for the offensive. The strength of the Soviets dwarfed their enemy: Army Group North Ukraine comprised two panzer armies and the First Hungarian Army, with some 420 tanks and self-propelled guns, and various other vehicles thrown into the mix. The newly appointed General Josef Harpe, who had replaced Model who was needed in Army Group Center, hastily managed to commit 400,000 troops supported by 700 aircraft.

German commanders were fully aware of the dire consequences in the Ukraine if they were defeated. They appreciated that if the Soviets succeeded it would undoubtedly prize wide open the door to Poland and then Germany. Hitler told his front-line commanders

An artillery observation post. An SS officer is using the 6x30 Sf.14Z Scherefernrohr or scissor binoculars searching for enemy targets. Each artillery battery had an observation post among the front-line positions. (NARA)

that the troops must improve their present positions and stand and fight. In March 1944, Hitler had been obsessed with his new *Fester Platz* or Fortified Area order. These fortified areas were established in a number of Russian and Ukrainian cities and were manned by determined German forces ordered to stem the Red Army onslaught with fanatical defense. In Hitler's eyes, if he could hold back the Red Army in the Ukraine, this would prevent the Soviets using the southern sector as a springboard into Poland. The war in the East could then be drawn out into a longer battle of attrition and stagnate once more for a fourth Russian winter.

Along the Army Group North Ukraine front soldiers were slowly becoming aware of the looming danger. As German intelligence monitored increased enemy activity, the troops prepared their positions the best they could with what limited materiel and supplies they had at their disposal.

During the early hours of July 13, the morning was suddenly broken by the shouts of Soviet gunnery officers from the 1st Ukrainian Front giving the order for their men to open a massive artillery barrage across the defensive positions of Army Group North

A Waffen-SS Panther crew pose for the camera.

Ukraine. Thousands of guns, mortars, and Katyusha multiple rocket launchers poured fire and destruction onto the German positions. Then massed Soviet tanks and infantry went into action attacking the junction of the First and Fourth Panzer Armies. The German 357th Infantry Division, 349th Infantry Division, the SS Freiwillge (Volunteer) Division Galizien, and the III Panzer Corps—particularly the 8th Panzer Division—tried to stem the onslaught. However, Soviet firepower was overwhelming and the 1st Ukrainian Front was able to take ground and advance on the towns of Sasiv and Zolochiv.

A few days later heavy Soviet attacks westward forced a gap toward Lvov as advanced spearheads made their way to the town of Busk. As a result of the fast-moving infantry and tank columns, Soviet units including the 3rd Guards Tank Army managed to encircle 45,000 men of XIII Army Corps near Brody. In spite of a number of desperate attempts by understrength and exhausted panzer units to relieve the Brody *kessel*, the troops inside

Utilising a damaged building for concealment is an Elefant tank destroyer which was part of the 653rd Heavy *Panzerjäger* Battalion. By August 1944 with mounting losses the 653rd was withdrawn to refit in Kraków. It remained on the Eastern Front, as part of 17th Army, and was redesignated the 614th Heavy *Panzerjäger* Company.

A Panther crew, part of an ad hoc unit in the First Panzer Army, during a pause in the fighting. The First Panzer Army defended Lvov and its front to the south, but had neither the manpower nor weaponry to effectively hold the city.

An Sd.Kfz.251 halftrack personnel carrier operating east of Lvov in the final days of the Soviet campaign.

were trapped and help was futile. As a result of this encirclement, a 170-mile breach was created along Army Group North Ukraine's front. In desperation, General Harpe ordered a withdrawal of his forces to avoid a similar fate at Brody. With massive artillery and aerial bombardments, the 1st Ukrainian Front inflicted heavy casualties as German units hastily retreated across open terrain. The scene was one of complete panic and disorder as Harpe's army group fell back. The Fourth Panzer Army retreated towards the Vistula River and the First Panzer Army along with First Hungarian Army withdrew toward the Carpathian Mountains to hold the city of Lvov.

During the last week of July, the Soviets rolled across the ravaged countryside of the Ukraine into Poland and through the shattered German front. On July 24, the First Panzer Army prepared to defend Lvov and its front to the south, but it had neither the manpower nor adequate weapons to effectively fight for the city. As a result, two days later, Soviet forces began advancing into the suburbs. What was left of the First Panzer Army then began withdrawing to avoid complete annihilation. The city fell with relative ease. With the fall of Lvov, the Germans had been completely forced out of Western Ukraine, and Konev could now attack across the Vistula with the objective of capturing the city of Sandomierz in German-held southern Poland.

On July 29, the 1st Ukrainian Front renewed its offensive with Konev's spearheads quickly reaching the Vistula and establishing a substantial bridgehead near Baranow Sandomierski. Over the next couple of days, fighting in the area was fierce, with German divisions fighting to the bitter end trying to slow the Soviet onslaught and prevent the expansion of further Soviet bridgeheads.

On July 26 Soviet forces entered the suburbs of Lvov and the city fell with relative ease. Here T-34 tanks advance along ul.Kazimierzowska in the city following its capture.

In early August, the German front temporarily stabilized as Soviet units halted after outstripping their supply lines. Whilst Konev's forces regrouped, Army Group North Ukraine was given no less than 10 divisions transferred from Army Group South Ukraine. These included one panzer division, three Hungarian divisions, six StuG brigades and the 501st Heavy Tank Battalion equipped with Tiger IIs. These divisions were hastily thrown into defensive positions around Sandomierz.

With these new replacements the Germans were able to launch a large-scale counterattack back across the Vistula using the towns of Mielec and Tarnobrzeg as fortified defensive areas. The Soviets were outnumbered and incurred high losses along the river. However, in spite of the casualties, by August 16, the German attacks began to wither and Soviet units were able to repulse a number of German assaults, causing substantial losses to the Wehrmacht armor. As a result, the 1st Ukrainian Front was able to smash open the German lines, which forced Army Group North Ukraine to withdraw from Sandomierz. The city was then captured and the Lvov–Sandomierz Offensive ended with complete success for the Soviets, in spite of the horrendous casualties.

In Profile:
76mm Divisional Gun M1942 (ZiS-3) & 122mm Howitzer M1938 (M-30)

76mm Divisional Gun M1942 (ZiS-3), Lvov, July 25, 1944

The ZiS-3 had good anti-armor capabilities. Its armor-piercing round could knock out German vehicles such as the Marder and Wespe. However, frontal armor of later tanks, like the Tiger I and later Panther, were immune to this weapon. This gun is painted in its original Soviet color of olive green. (Oliver Missing)

122mm Howitzer M1938 (M-30), Sandomierz, July 26, 1944

By 1944, an artillery regiment of a typical Soviet rifle division was armed with 36 122mm howitzers, primarily employed against field fortifications, for clearing minefields and for breaching barbed wire. This weapon is in an elevated position and is painted in its original Soviet color of olive green. (Oliver Missing)

Vistula–Oder Offensive, January–February 1945

Following the successful Lvov–Sandomierz Offensive, the situation on the German front was dire. Konev's 1st Ukrainian Front was now in Poland, pulling up to the Vistula River. Farther south, Petrov's 4th Ukrainian Front had advanced through the Carpathians on a line from the Tartar Pass to the Lupkov before racing into Ruthenia and then west into Slovakia. Simultaneously, Malinovsky's 2nd Ukrainian Front had swept aside powerful German defenses and reached the Bulgarian border in early September.

Soviet troops then reached the Yugoslav frontier, and on September 8, Bulgaria and Romania declared war on Germany. By September 23, Soviet forces arrived at the Hungarian border and immediately made for the Danube, finally reaching the river to the south of Budapest.

It was here in Hungary that Hitler placed the utmost importance of defending what he called the last bastion of defense in the East. Against all military logic, the Führer felt that it was Hungary and not the Vistula River in Poland, which presented a natural

SS-Reichsführer Heinrich Himmler, right, confers with an officer. Hitler bestowed on Himmler command of the Vistula Front in a drastic effort to halt the Soviet advance. However, Himmler lacked any kind of military expertise. (NARA)

A column of whitewashed Soviet ISU-122 heavy self-propelled tank destroyers during an advance through western Ukraine.

barrier against an advance on Germany. For the defense of Hungary, he was determined to use his premier Waffen-SS divisions, including Totenkopf and Wiking that were positioned along the Vistula River. By transferring these premier SS divisions, he significantly deprived the defense of Poland.

The defense of the Vistula was now left to General Harpe's Army Group A which consisted of three armies: the Ninth Army deployed around Warsaw, the Fourth Panzer Army positioned on the Vistula bend in the Baranow salient, and the Seventeenth Army to the south. In total the group was comprised of 450,000 troops, 1,150 tanks and assault guns, and 4,000 artillery pieces.

A whitewashed 15cm field howitzer is prepared for a fire mission in its elevated position. This gun was primarily designed to attack targets deeper in the enemy's rear.

A 10.5cm leFH 18/42 infantry gun crew in action. Throughout the war the 10.5cm gun provided the Heer and Waffen-SS with a versatile, relatively mobile, base of fire. Even during the last months of the war, experience showed that artillery support was of decisive importance in both defensive and offensive roles.

In front of Harpe stood two massive Soviet armies: the 1st Belorussian Front was positioned around Warsaw which had secured two strategically important bridgeheads at Magnuszew and Pulawy, and occupying the Sandomierz bridgehead was the 1st Ukrainian Front. Between them they had 163 divisions of over two million soldiers, 7,500 tanks and assault guns, and 16,000 artillery pieces including Katyusha multiple rocket launchers.

Dwarfed by the strength of the Red Army there was real concern in the field by German commanders that they could not hold back the enemy. By December 1944, German intelligence began receiving disturbing reports that Soviet armor was on the move in what was believed to preparation for a new winter offensive. Days later there were strong indications that infantry divisions and artillery were massing opposite the German army group. By the end of the first week of January 1945, two Soviet armies were identified facing Army Group A.

Early on the morning of January 12, 1945, the 1st Ukrainian Front opened with a massive preparatory ground and aerial bombardment along the Baranow bridgehead to soften up some of the strongest defensive positions. Some of these defensive lines comprised intricate mazes of blockhouses and trenches. Towns and villages that fell in the path of these defensive belts were evacuated. Thousands of women, children, and old men were removed from their dwellings and many were actually pressed into service to help construct antitank ditches and other obstacles.

In Profile:
7.5cm PaK 40 & Marder II, Sd.Kfz.132

7.5cm PaK 40, Defense of the Oder, January 1945

The 7.5cm PaK 40 became the workhorse of infantry antitank units on the Eastern Front. It was the most widely used antitank gun in the Wehrmacht. It was capable of penetrating frontal armor of most Soviet tanks, and deadly to all of them from the flanks and rear. If properly used by a well-trained crew, this PaK gun could be employed to supplement divisional field artillery. (Oliver Missing)

Marder II, Sd.Kfz.132, March 1945, Oder Front

The Marder II was a German tank destroyer, a converted mobile antitank gun bolted onto a Pz.Kpfw.II chassis. There were two versions: the first mounted a modified Soviet 7.62cm gun (Sd.Kfz.132) firing German ammunition, while the other mounted the German 7.5cm PaK 40 gun (Sd.Kfz.131). These vehicles were mainly found in the *Panzerjäger Abteilungen*—tank-destroyer battalions—of the panzer divisions, but by 1945 what were left of them were found in ad hoc units in defensive positions. (Oliver Missing)

German Order of Battle
ARMY GROUP A

Commander: Josef Harpe; from January 20, 1945 Ferdinand Schörner

NINTH ARMY

LVI Panzer Corps

XXXXVI Panzer Corps

VIII Corps

FOURTH PANZER ARMY

XLII Corps

XXIV Panzer Corps

XLVIII Panzer Corps

SEVENTEENTH ARMY

LIX Corps

XI Corps

XI SS Panzer Corps

Winter-clad grenadiers march in the snow supported by a Sturmgeschütz. The soldier in the foreground is armed with a Panzerfaust.

Red Army Order of Battle

1ST BELORUSSIAN FRONT

Commander: Georgy Zhukov

47th Army

1st Polish Army

3rd Shock Army

61st Army

1st Guards Tank Army

2nd Guards Tank Army

5th Shock Army

8th Guards Army

69th Army

33rd Army

1ST UKRAINIAN FRONT

Commander: Ivan Konev

21st Army

6th Army

3rd Guards Army

13th Army

4th Tank Army

3rd Guards Tank Army

1st Guards Cavalry Corps

52nd Army

5th Guards Army

59th Army

60th Army

The Soviet infantry and armored assault was fast and fierce and over the course of the first day of the offensive Red Army units encircled units of the Fourth Panzer Army defending the smoldering town of Kielce. Within two days the 1st Ukrainian Front forced a crossing over the Nida River, and began threatening German positions in front of the town of Radomsko on the Warta River.

To the north of Konev the 1st Belorussian Front opened up a large-scale attack along the Magnuszew and Puławy bridgeheads. The 5th Shock and 8th Guards Armies broke out of the Magnuszew bridgehead and fought a number of hard-pressed battles against determined German opposition. The 1st and 2nd Guards Tank Armies were then committed to battle and drove the Germans from their devastated lines. The Ninth Army frantically tried to conduct a number of local counterattacks, but could not withstand the weight of Soviet firepower and the units were either destroyed or forced to withdraw.

The offensive was overwhelming and the front simply buckled under the sheer firepower of the enemy. Huge parts of the German defense crumbled and large areas of southern Poland were quickly captured. Within days the city of Radom was liberated by the 69th Army while the 2nd Guards Tank Army attacked toward Sochaczew. Simultaneously,

Soviet tankmen pore over a map during the Vistula–Oder Offensive, January 1945.

A German 15cm sIG 33 howitzer ready for action.

Two Tiger tanks with panzergrenadiers getting a ride to the front.

A battery of elevated 15cm howitzers ready for action along the Vistula–Oder front. These heavy field guns could hurl their destructive charge miles into the enemy lines.

A column of T-34 tanks halted in a heavily defended town. Most of the riflemen have not dismounted, using the turrets as protection against enemy fire.

An Sd.Kfz.7/1 half-tracked tractor armed with a 2cm Flakvierling 38 antiaircraft gun system. Some 120 boxes of ammunition with 20 rounds each for a total of 2,400 rounds were carried; 30 were carried in the vehicle itself, with the other 90 in the trailer.

Panzergrenadiers armed with an assortment of weaponry including a Panzerfaust next to a stationary whitewashed Tiger tank in the snow.

A battery of Wespe self-propelled howitzers with their 10.5cm 18 guns in an elevated position preparing for a fire mission.

A whitewashed Wespe self-propelled howitzer being prepared for action during operations in the winter of 1944.

the 1st Guards Tank Army raced to seize bridgeheads over the Pilica and attack towards Łódź.

The repercussions meant that Warsaw was now threatened. The Soviet 47th Army had crossed the Vistula and advanced at breakneck speed to Warsaw from the north, while the 61st and 1st Polish Armies encircled the Polish capital from the south. Warsaw fell on January 17, as Army Group A headquarters issued orders for the city to be abandoned. Units of the 2nd Guards and 3rd Shock Armies entered the devastated city.

With Warsaw captured the German front receded and units hurriedly retreated before being completely annihilated. On the Oder River the strategic town of Breslau was now threatened by Konev's forces. The town had been turned into a fortress and defended by various Volkssturm, Hitlerjugend, Waffen-SS, and ad-hoc units from the 269th Infantry Division. Breslau was the gateway to the industrial heartland of Upper Silesia. The Soviet plan was to encircle the area and annihilate the German Seventeenth Army which had over the course of the previous six months withdrawn from the Crimea, and limped into Upper Silesia. The army lacked meaningful armor and weaponry and defenses were inadequate. The Soviet 21st, 59th and 60th Armies took advantage of the German army's weak position and were tasked with its encirclement.

On January 17 the 59th and 60th Armies began the encirclement by driving head-on into the German positions, fighting a number of battles as it advanced. With German units drawn off to contest the two Soviet armies, the Soviet 21st Army then quickly maneuvered to the north, while at the same time the 3rd Guards Tank Army attacked toward Breslau

A Russian machine-gun crew with a captured MG 34 machine gun sited on a sled.

Grenadiers wearing winter reversibles and armed with their Karbiner 98K bolt action rifles march through the snow as they withdraw through southern Ukraine towards the Polish frontier.

A smiling young T-34 tanker tucks into some rations whilst his vehicle is concealed in foliage in a forest.

and then swung south along the upper Oder, thereby cutting off the Seventeenth Army. Some 100,000 troops were now trapped around Katowice, and after repeated requests for a breakout, the remnants of the Seventeenth Army broke out during the night of January 27.

By this time, with the German front totally exposed, Konev's northern flank comprising the 4th Tank Army advanced to the Oder and secured a major bridgehead at Steinau. At the same time the 1st Belorussian Front's 2nd Guards Tank Army also advanced to the Oder, while to the south the 8th Guards Army reached Łódź and captured it on January 19.

On January 25, Hitler renamed the remnants of Army Group A Army Group Vistula. By combining the two army groups he hoped that it would give the front more cohesion. He also needed to protect Berlin against the Soviet advance from the Vistula. Hitler bestowed none other than SS-Reichsführer Heinrich Himmler to command the Vistula Front. However, Himmler lacked any kind of military knowledge or expertise and relied on his staff and commanders in the field to direct operations; he seldom ventured from his headquarters train and barely visited the battlefield.

The situation was dire. German defense had largely collapsed and the Red Army was unstoppable. The 2nd Guards Tank and 5th Shock Armies reached the Oder almost unopposed.

Volkssturm troops defending the Oder. Army Group Vistula was positioned behind the threatened front and consisted mainly of Volkssturm units and militia too young or old to serve in the regular army. Along this weak front, a number of volunteer SS units and ad hoc panzer formations bolstered the understrength and undertrained forces, but resources were too limited to impede the Soviet onslaught.

Farther south, Konev's forces made equal progress capturing the city of Kraków and driving westward, mopping up retreating Heer and Waffen-SS troops as they swept through towns and villages.

On January 31, the Soviet offensive was halted in order for its troops to regroup and prepare for the final offensive, against the Reich capital itself, only 43 miles away. A number of strategically important bridgeheads had been successfully achieved along the Oder. What followed now, over a period of weeks, was to wait until the ice thawed, which would turn the fields and roads into a morass of mud. The Soviet supply lines too had been stretched to the limit, so units waited to be resupplied before resumption of operations west of the Oder and onto Berlin.

A portrait photo of General Gotthard Heinrici. As the Vistula front collapsed, Hitler held Himmler responsible and accused him of disobeying orders. As a result of these failures, the Reichsführer's military career ended on March 20, 1945 when Hitler replaced him with Heinrici.

In Profile:
ISU-152 & ISU-122

ISU-152, Vistula Front, January 1945

The ISU-152 was a heavy assault gun and an extremely valuable weapon in urban combat operations, especially during assaults into Berlin in April 1945. During its advance from the Vistula to the Oder, to minimize the risks of being knocked out by deadly German Panzerfaust units, the ISU-152 usually acted in one- or two-vehicle detachments alongside infantry squads for protection. This was common especially during urbanized assaults. This vehicle is probably finished in its original Soviet color of olive green. (Oliver Missing)

ISU-122, Oder River, February 1945

The ISU-122 was used as a powerful assault gun, a self-propelled howitzer, and a long-range tank destroyer. For urban combat, this vehicle was utilized as an assault gun with deadly effect. This vehicle is probably finished in its original Soviet color of olive green. (Oliver Missing)

Defeat, February–March 1945

Following the successful conclusion of the Soviet Vistula–Oder Offensive, the military situation along the front between Berlin and the Oder stagnated through February 1945. Most German units were awaiting resupplies and trying to regroup as losses had been high. According to Soviet sources operations undertaken by the 1st Ukrainian and Belorussian Fronts during the Vistula–Oder Offensive alone had resulted in the deaths of 150,000 German troops.

While the Germans were able to make good some of the losses through measures such as the mass mobilization of the Volkssturm, Army Group A and then Army Group Vistula had clearly suffered significant losses as a result of the Red Army offensives in January 1945. Whilst still licking its wounds, Army Group Vistula fought a series of defensive and offensive battles in order to relieve areas encircled or cut off.

Himmler infused little hope into his field commanders about the army group's defensive strategy. Most had few illusions about what the Reichsführer could accomplish as a military commander, believing his sole purpose was to buy time for Berlin. Himmler relied heavily on his new Chief of Staff, General Walther Wenck, who was more or less running the army

Red Army antitank rifle position during winter operations in 1945. By early February German forces in the East had been driven back to the Oder River, the last bastion of defense before Berlin. Only three weeks earlier, the Eastern Front was still deep in Poland.

Winter-clad Luftwaffe ground troops thrown into the defense in the East.

group anyhow. Wenck was regarded a capable commander and a brilliant improviser. He was given the task of launching an offensive in February known as Operation *Solstice*, or the Stargard tank battle as it became known. The offensive was to relieve the city of Kustrin and was launched on February 15 from Stargard in Pomerania. Three corps of the Eleventh SS Panzer Army were deployed. Astonishingly, a considerable number of armored vehicles were allocated to the offensive, but no trains were available to transport them. Instead, the panzers, assault guns, halftracks, and an assortment of other fighting vehicles had to make the arduous and perilous journey from one part of the front to another. Most did not arrive in time and, due to serious shortages, only three days' ammunition and fuel were immediately available to the Waffen-SS and supporting Heer and Luftwaffe ground units. When the attack was launched much of the armor still had not arrived, so the Germans fought on with what they had available.

Troops moving from one part of the front to another in order to help strengthen areas buckling under the sheer weight of the Soviet onslaught. The one German in the middle of the line appears to have stumbled.

The moment a 15cm howitzer is fired and recoiled. One of the gunners plugs his ears to the deafening boom.

However, within three days, Zhukov's 1st Belorussian Front had ground down the German assaults and brought the offensive to a halt, forcing the remnants to withdraw. As a consequence, further attacks against Kustrin were called off, but this did not prevent German units from launching other attacks in East Pomerania, taking advantage of the high casualty rates in the Red Army. The 1st Belorussian Front, for example, had suffered serious

Probably a Russian soldier clad in his winter whites taking cover from behind a knocked-out Pz.Kpfw.IV. The soldier is armed with the PPSh-41 sub machine gun.

A well-protected Pz.Kpfw.Ausf.H during winter operations in 1944. Note all the additional track links bolted to the tank's armored plating.

A Soviet colonel and a very young tanker, no more than a boy, pose next to a captured German Sd.Kfz.10. The Soviet star is painted on the side of the vehicle for recognition purposes.

117

War-weary grenadiers at the front. Along 200 miles of the remaining defensive front, pockets of antitank and artillery guns were strung out in haphazard fashion, almost totally unprotected.

losses during the Vistula–Oder Offensive: between January 12 and February 3, 1945, it had suffered some 77,000 casualties. To make matters worse the Soviets had a number of supply bottlenecks, coupled with increased Luftwaffe activity making troop concentration and counterattacks difficult. Yet, in spite of the losses and logistical problems, Zhukov initiated a series of counterattacks aimed at stalling Army Group Vistula and preventing the enemy gaining further ground. This also included neutralizing urban centers that were part of

In grim weather a Soviet tank passes a knocked-out Sturmgeschütz on its way to the Seelow Heights.

Soviet troops inspecting a knocked-out Panther tank during the advance to the Oder.

Preparing for the final showdown along the Oder. A Soviet tankman tucks into his rations next to his well-concealed T-34 tank.

A soldier is about to clamber out of the rear hatch of the Panzerwerfer launch vehicle. Note the 15cm Nebewerfer-Zehnling 42 launcher mounted on the roof. The tubes could traverse 360° and fire 10 15cm high explosives.

Hitler's "Fortified Area" policy to further reduce the cohesion of German defenses. Though these renewed Soviet attacks were successful, Army Group Vistula had actually delayed the planned Red Army offensive against Berlin by two months, until April.

By March the situation for the army group was desperate in spite of fanatical resistance. Konev's forces managed to clear Upper Silesia, and on March 15 attacked south of Grottkau

A Pz.Kpfw.IV knocked out during a defensive action in southern Poland.

and west of the bridgehead north of Ratobor. At the same time the 4th Ukrainian Front pushed through Slovakia. On March 17 Konev's two pincers linked up, encircling the LVI Panzer Corps southwest of Oppeln. The German front began to collapse. Himmler found himself under constant pressure from his Führer who continuously telephoned him about the military situation which was fast deteriorating. Unable to provide coherent reports, coupled with failures to counterattack against the growing might of the Red Army, Hitler held Himmler responsible for the demise of Army Group Vistula's position and accused him of disobeying orders. As a result, Himmler's military career ended on March 20, 1945, when Hitler replaced him with General Gotthard Heinrici.

By the time Heinrici took over command from Himmler the army group was in a parlous condition. At his disposal he had two armies, the Third Panzer Army and the Ninth Army, which were tasked with preventing the Soviets from attacking across the Oder. However, the Germans had serious manpower and materiel shortages and had to rely on the terrain itself. As a result, units from the Ninth Army were ordered to dig in with three defensive lines atop the Seelow Heights overlooking the Oder.

It was now a waiting game for Army Group Vistula. They were aware the offensive against Berlin would come at any time. As for the Soviets, they were preparing a mighty force for the final offensive. In spite of the significant losses incurred during their often

A column of Red Army T-34/85 tanks advance along a road bound for the Oder.

Waffen-SS MG 42 machine-gun crew during a defensive action. By this period of the war a German report noted that for every mile of front some remaining regiments had one artillery piece, one heavy machine gun, two light machine guns and about 150 men. For every two and a half miles of front they had, in addition, one antitank gun. For every four miles they had one panzer, and for every six miles one battalion.

hazardous and dangerous advance to the Oder, the Red Army had achieved remarkable success. From the days of launching its troops across the Dnieper River in the Ukraine in late 1943, battling across the Crimea in the spring of 1944, to driving its powerful spearheads during the Lvov–Sandomierz Offensive, and then advancing to the banks of the Oder for the final assault on Berlin, the crushing of Army Group South was complete and absolute, but it had taken almost two years of hell and sacrifice.

A column of T-34 tanks pauses during the drive to the Oder.

| Epilogue

No war in history is comparable to the magnitude of sacrifice of the men and women who were embroiled on the Eastern Front. By the time the war in Russia had started to turn in favor of the Red Army during the summer of 1943, millions of Soviet soldiers and civilians had perished. The Red Army slowly adapted to offensive operations, whilst the Germans were forced to diversify on the battlefield and switch to a fighting withdrawal and a defensive posture until the eventual demise of the Third Reich.

Nowhere was this stratagem more highlighted than on the German southern front between 1943 and 1945. It is evident that the Soviets learned from their mistakes and were able to adapt quickly and decisively on the battlefield, even if it meant sacrificing thousands of soldiers and weaponry to win a position. The Soviets were able to deploy massive concentrations of men and firepower to saturate an area in order to win at any cost.

As for the German war machine, its armies struggled to maintain structure against an overwhelming foe. The lack of troops and weaponry played a significant part in their demise. In addition, they received insufficient reinforcements from other parts of the front and the Reich, and were often unable to fight cohesively. Another contributing factor to defeat was deception. Hitler had been duped into believing the Soviet summer offensive would come in the south, and not the center. So, he ordered that vital equipment and resources be stripped from Army Group Center to create a reserve to strike a preemptive blow in North Ukraine. As a result, Army Group Center lost most of its panzers, a quarter of its self-propelled guns, half its antitank capability, and over a quarter of its heavy artillery.

When Operation *Bagration* was launched, the Soviets quickly gained the initiative. As the German center buckled and fell apart, chaotic and irrational orders ensued, calling on essential supplies and weaponry to be rushed from the south to the center, putting additional pressure on the southern front and depriving units of critical men and materiel. When the center finally collapsed, the Soviets were able to concentrate four massive fronts against the south.

Losses on both sides were staggering. Between August 1943 and February 1945 1.1 million German soldiers were killed or wounded. The Red Army losses were far greater during this period: some 3.6 million troops were killed, wounded, or missing.

With nothing but a trail of devastation in its wake, the Soviet Army began its preparations along the Oder to commence the battle for Berlin. They had waited for almost two years for this final victory. It had been a long journey from the Dnieper to the gates of the Reich capital, covering almost 2,000 miles. But finally, the Germans were vanquished forever; the Soviet destruction of Army Group South was complete.

| Further Reading

Adair, Paul (2004) [1994]. *Hitler's Greatest Defeat: The Collapse of Army Group Center, June 1944*. London: Weidenfeld Military.

Beevor, Antony; Vinogradova, Luba, eds. (2006). *A Writer at War: Vasily Grossman With the Red Army*. London: Pimlico.

Bishop, Chris, ed. (2002). *The Encyclopedia of Weapons of World War II*. New York: Metro Books.

Buttar, Prit (2020). The Reckoning: *The Defeat of Army Group South, 1944*. Oxford, England: Osprey Publishing.

Dear, I. C. B. & Foot, M. R. D. (eds.) (1995). *The Oxford Guide to World War II*. New York, N.Y.: Oxford University Press.

DiNardo, Richard (2005). *Germany and the Axis Powers: From Coalition to Collapse*. Lawrence, K.S.: University Press of Kansas.

Dunn, Walter S. (2000). *Soviet Blitzkrieg: The Battle for White Russia, 1944*. Boulder, C.O.: Lynne Rienner.

A battery of Soviet artillery prepares to open the assault on Berlin. By April 1945 the atmosphere among the troops of Army Group Vistula was a mix of terrible foreboding and despair as the Soviets prepared to push forward from the Oder. For the attack the Red Army had mustered some 2.5 million men, in four armies, supported by 41,600 guns and heavy mortars, and 6,250 tanks and self-propelled guns.

Forczyk, Robert (2007). *Panther vs. T-34: Ukraine 1943*. Oxford, England: Osprey Publishing.

Fritz, Stephen G. (1995). *Frontsoldaten: The German Soldier in World War II*. Lexington, K.Y.: University Press of Kentucky.

Fritz, Stephen G. (2011). *Ostkrieg: Hitler's War of Extermination in the East*. Lexington, K.Y.: University Press of Kentucky.

Glantz, David. M. (ed.) (2004). *Byelorussia 1944–The Soviet General Staff Study*. Oxford, England: Routledge.

Glantz, David M. (2007). *Red Storm over the Balkans: The Failed Soviet Invasion of Romania, Spring 1944*. Lawrence, K.S.: University Press of Kansas.

Kehrig, Manfred (1974). *Stalingrad*. Stuttgart: Deutsche Verlags Anstalt.

Krivosheev, G. F. (1997). *Soviet Casualties and Combat Losses in the Twentieth Century*. London: Greenhill Books.

Lyons, Michael J. (1999). *World War II: A Short History*. Upper Saddle River, N.J.: Prentice Hall.

Mazower, Mark (2008). *Hitler's Empire: Nazi Rule in Occupied Europe*. London: Allen Lane.

Merridale, C. (2006). *Ivan's War: Inside the Red Army, 1939–45*. London: Faber & Faber.

Militärgeschichtliches Forschungsamt (Military History Research Office), Federal Republic of Germany (1979–2008). *Das Deutsche Reich und der Zweite Weltkrieg* (tr. *The German Reich and the Second World War*) Vol. 13. Stuttgart: Deutsche Verlags-Anstalt.

Mitcham, S. (2007). *German Defeat in the East 1944–45*. Mechanicsburg, P.A.: Stackpole Books.

Niepold, Gerd (1987). *Battle for White Russia: The Destruction of Army Group Center, June 1944*. London: Brassey's Defence Publishers.

Seaton, Albert (1971). *The Russo-German War, 1941–1945*. London: Arthur Barker.

Stahel, David (2009). *Operation Barbarossa and Germany's Defeat in the East*. Cambridge & New York: Cambridge University Press.

Tieke, Wilhelm (2001). *Tragedy of the Faithful: A History of the III. (germanisches) SS-Panzer-Korps*. Winnipeg: J. J. Fedorowicz.

Zetterling, Niklas & Franksson, Anders (1998). "Analyzing World War II Eastern Front Battles." *The Journal of Slavic Military Studies*. Oxford, England: Routledge.

Ziemke, Earl F. (1968). *Stalingrad to Berlin: The German Defeat in the East*. Washington, D.C.: Office of the Chief of Military History, U.S. Army.

Ziemke, Earl F. & Bauer, Magna E. (1987). *Moscow to Stalingrad: Decision in the East*. Washington, D.C.: Center of Military History, U.S. Army.

Index